US INTELLIGENCE COMMUNITY REFORM STUDIES SINCE 1947

MICHAEL WARNER
J. KENNETH MCDONALD

Strategic Management Issues Office

Center *for the* Study *of* Intelligence
Washington, DC

April 2005

Executive Summary

The publication of *The 9/11 Commission Report*, the war in Iraq, and subsequent negotiation of the Intelligence Reform and Terrorism Prevention Act of 2004 have provoked the most intense debate over the future of American intelligence since the end of World War II. For observers of this national discussion—as well as of future debates that are all but inevitable—this paper offers a historical perspective on reform studies and proposals that have appeared over the course of the US Intelligence Community's evolution into its present form.

We have examined the origins, context, and results of 14 significant official studies that have surveyed the American intelligence system since 1947. We explore the reasons these studies were launched, the recommendations they made, and the principal results that they achieved. It should surprise no one that many of the issues involved—such as the institutional relationships between military and civilian intelligence leaders—remain controversial to the present time. For this reason, we have tried both to clarify the perennial issues that arise in intelligence reform efforts and to determine those factors that favor or frustrate their resolution. Of the 14 reform surveys we examined, only the following achieved substantial success in promoting the changes they proposed: the Dulles Report (1949), the Schlesinger Report (1971), the Church Committee Report (1976), and the 9/11 Commission Report (2004).

The earliest such study, the January 1949 Dulles Report, achieved its considerable influence only after a disastrous warning failure almost 18 months later at the outset of the Korean War. A new Director of Central Intelligence (DCI), Lt. Gen. Walter Bedell Smith, used this report to make major changes at the Central Intelligence Agency. While organizing the CIA into a durable internal structure, Smith also formed the Board of National Estimates to coordinate and produce National Intelligence Estimates (NIEs), created new offices for current intelligence and research, and took control of the Agency's expanding covert action campaign. Most importantly, DCI Smith shaped the nation's disparate intelligence agencies into something recognizable as an Intelligence Community—a term first used during his tenure. He maneuvered the Department of State and the Joint Chiefs of Staff out of clandestine operations, and pushed successfully to bring the signals intelligence capabilities of the armed services under civilian control.

Almost 20 years later, as the Vietnam War wound down in 1971, James R. Schlesinger of the Office of Management and Budget (and later DCI) produced a review of the Intelligence Community for President Nixon and the National Security Council (NSC). While the cost of intelligence had exploded over the past decade, Schlesinger observed, the community had failed to achieve "a commensurate improvement in the scope and overall quantity of intelligence products." A manager was needed to plan and rationalize intelligence collection and evaluate its product, both within the Defense Department and across the Intelligence Community. This manager, he explained, could be made anything from a new coordinator in the White House to a full-fledged ""Director of National Intelligence" controlling the budgets and personnel of the entire community. Since Schlesinger outlined the concept in 1971, the need for a Director of National Intelligence has been a recurring theme in intelligence reform studies.

The Watergate scandal and President Nixon's 1974 resignation forestalled full adoption of Schlesinger's recommendations, but his report nevertheless prompted significant changes. These included the creation of a staff to help the DCI manage "Community Affairs," the appointment of an Assistant Secretary of Defense for Intelligence, and the merger of the armed services' cryptologic organizations into a Central Security Service under the National Security Agency (NSA). In the years since President Nixon's November 1971 response to Schlesinger's Report, every DCI has been expected to oversee the preparation of the Intelligence Community's budgets, to establish intelligence requirements and priorities, and to ensure the quality of its products.

The investigation of US intelligence by Senator Frank Church's committee in 1975, which focused largely on the CIA, marked another watershed. It concluded that the United States could be well served by its capability for clandestine activities overseas and covert action operations—with proper safeguards. More importantly, it altered the relationship of the Intelligence Community to Congress. The Senate and House soon formed permanent committees to oversee the Intelligence Community, which made it more accountable to the legislative branch. While these two committees have always operated within distinct limits, in part because of their competition with the established authorizing and appropriating committees, their oversight has had a clearly positive effect. By looking at the Intelligence Community more or less as a whole, they have tended to make it more coherent, disciplined, and accountable.

The attacks of 11 September 2001 prompted new calls for high-level investigations and far-reaching reforms. Indeed, the 9/11 Commission's Report (published in July 2004) was almost certainly the most influential of any of the surveys examined here, in that it precipitated sweeping amendments to the National Security Act of 1947. Some of its suggestions echoed those of earlier surveys: the DCI's duties, for instance, should be split between a chief of the Intelligence Community and a director of the CIA. President Bush quickly adopted several of the 9/11 Commission Report's proposals, signing four Executive Orders on intelligence and related issues, but Congress soon went further still by enacting the "Intelligence Reform and Terrorism Prevention Act" in December 2004. That Act incorporated the precept that American intelligence needed a new sort of coordinator: a "Director of National Intelligence" (DNI) who would manage the planning, policy, and budgets of the community across the full range of intelligence, foreign and domestic. This did away with the position of Director of Central Intelligence and—by bridging the old foreign-domestic divide—adjusted one of the compromises struck in drafting the original National Security Act in 1947.

Having examined these and other surveys of the Intelligence Community, we recognize that much of the change since 1947 has been more ad hoc than systematically planned. The political impetus to commission a thorough study when contemplating change is nevertheless almost inexorable. Our investigation indicates that to bring about significant change, a study commission has had to get two things right: process and substance.

With respect to process, political sponsorship is important. Two studies that had large and comparatively rapid effects—the 1949 Dulles Report and the 1971 Schlesinger Report—were both sponsored by the National Security Council. The 9/11 Commission, with its public hearings in the midst of an election season, had even more impact, while the Church Committee's effects were indirect but eventually powerful. It's perhaps worth noting that a study commission whose chairman later became DCI, as in the case of Allen Dulles and James Schlesinger, is also likely to have a lasting influence. Finally, studies conducted on the eve of or during a war, or in a war's immediate aftermath, are more likely to lead to change. The 1947 National Security Act drew lessons from World War II, and it was the outbreak of the Korean War in 1950 that brought about the intelligence reforms the Dulles Report had proposed over a year earlier. The 1971 Schlesinger Report responded to President Nixon's need to cut spending as he extracted the United States from the Vietnam War. The breakdown of the Cold War defense and foreign policy consensus during the Vietnam War set the scene for the Church Committee's investigations during 1975–76, but the fact that US troops were not in combat at the time certainly diminished the influence of its conclusions. In contrast, the 9/11 Commission Report was published at the height of a national debate over the War on Terror and the operations in Iraq, which magnified its salience.

Finally, in the substance of these reports, one large trend is evident over the years. Studies whose recommendations have caused power in the Intelligence Community to gravitate toward either the Director of Central Intelligence or the Office of the Secretary of Defense—or both—have generally had the most influence. This pattern of increasing concentration of intelligence power in the DCI and Secretary of Defense endured from the 1940s through the 1990s, whether Democrats or Republicans controlled the White House or Congress. Now that a DNI has replaced the DCI, it is not clear whether a similar trend will continue as the mission of defending the homeland against terrorism grows in importance. The Intelligence Reform and Terrorism Prevention Act of 2004 has changed the equation, making the new Director of National Intelligence institutionally almost equidistant between the Secretary of Defense and a new establishment coalescing around the homeland security mission. When a new pattern of influence and cooperation forms, we are confident that future reform surveys will not hesitate to propose ways to improve it.

Contents

Introduction

We shall attempt to explain why reform proposals recur so often, why they occasionally succeed, and why they often produce little change.

Since the beginning of World War II, presidents, members of Congress, military commanders, and a host of officials have puzzled over the uncertain scope and uneven performance of the US intelligence establishment. Periodically, especially in times of crisis, Congress and the executive have undertaken to reorganize it or redirect the path of its development. Proposals for reorganization and reform, however, sometimes show little knowledge or understanding of how intelligence agencies' capabilities have evolved over the years, how these agencies actually work, and how they fit together. To comprehend how the American intelligence structure functions as a system and how it has changed over time is a daunting task even for those who work in it. Inattention to the Intelligence Community's historical and institutional context may help explain why past efforts to reform it have more often than not produced only limited and fragmentary change.

To understand the Intelligence Community as it exists today thus requires some grounding in how it has evolved from World War II into its present complex, diffuse, and often bewildering form. It is this paper's purpose to explain the evolution of today's Intelligence Community by examining the principal reform efforts that various surveys, study commissions, and task forces have undertaken since 1947. Rather than offering a comprehensive history of the Intelligence Community's development or of the various surveys themselves, we hope to identify the principal study initiatives that influenced intelligence reform and the forms these changes followed.

From the initial proposals drafted at the end of World War II to the public reports after the Cold War's end in the 1990s, teams enjoying broad access to intelligence secrets and a mandate to appraise the American intelligence system have produced over a dozen studies. While almost all of these reports are now available in some declassified form, they have hardly ever been assembled and read together, either in their original state or in their public versions.[1] The importance of these studies does not rest solely on the effects they produced. Although a few—notably those spurred by a wartime crisis—have produced

---

[1] Richard A. Best, Jr., and Herbert A. Boerstling of the Congressional Research Service prepared one of the rare summaries of Intelligence Community studies. This work, "Proposals for Intelligence Reorganization, 1949–1996," is available in two versions. The first was reprinted in House Permanent Select Committee on Intelligence, "IC21: Intelligence Community in the 21st Century," 104th Congress, Second Session, 1996, 335ff. An updated revision was completed by CRS in July 2004; it summarized reform proposals since 1996. Appendix A of the Aspin-Brown Commission's final report has a briefer summary; see Commission on the Roles and Capabilities of the United States Intelligence Community, *Preparing for the 21st Century: An Appraisal of US Intelligence,* Washington, DC: Government Printing Office, 1996.

obvious results, the direct influence of others was much less.[2] The 1949 Dulles Report, for example, had a broad impact on the Intelligence Community's form and practice after the outbreak of the Korean War. Other similarly ambitious studies, however, have been largely ignored, because of either internal flaws or events beyond their authors' control. We shall attempt to explain why reform proposals recur so often, why they occasionally succeed, and why they often produce little change.

In a sense this monograph traces the history of the position of the Director of Central Intelligence. It begins with the challenges faced by the Truman administration and Congress when they struck the basic compromises that created the post of DCI, follows the evolution of the vision of centrally coordinated intelligence, and suggests why so many people at both ends of Pennsylvania Avenue felt in 2004 that a new system was needed. The debates have by no means ended with the passage of new legislation supplanting the DCI with a Director of National Intelligence. The issues that have been in play since 1946—and have been analyzed by virtually every survey of the intelligence establishment since then—will remain live ones for the foreseeable future. This study, by clarifying the past, may help inform discussions of how US intelligence can change to meet new challenges at a time when good intelligence has rarely been so important for our nation's future.

---

[2] Scott Harris reflected on "the track record of previous commissions in an effort to identify those factors that contributed to their success or failure" in "Effective Advisory Commissions: Insights from Historical Experience," RAND Project Memorandum 343-CRMAF, January 1995.

From Victory to Cold War: Three Decisions

Most nations do not combine intelligence functions in the way that President Truman did.

America acquired global responsibilities in World War II, but neither Congress nor the White House initially had a clear idea of how to discharge them. The ad hoc wartime measures that Franklin Roosevelt had undertaken before his death in April 1945 now needed to be evaluated with a critical eye. When he became President, Harry Truman reported later, one of his strongest convictions "was that the antiquated defense setup of the United States had to be reorganized quickly."[1] Similarly, in September 1945 the Joint Chiefs of Staff told Secretary of War Henry Stimson and Secretary of the Navy James Forrestal of the urgent need for intelligence reform:

> *Recent developments in the field of new weapons have advanced the question of an efficient intelligence service to a position of importance, vital to the security of the nation in a degree never attained and never contemplated in the past. It is now entirely possible that failure to provide such a system might bring national disaster.*[2]

The question was not whether to modernize intelligence but how. Each part of the Truman administration seemed to have its own ideas about the lessons of the war and the proper way for intelligence to support policymakers and commanders. Many of these ideas were mutually contradictory, and few officials had the insight and the clearances to see the full sweep of America's new capabilities. Nevertheless, in the beginning of 1946 the Truman administration made three crucial decisions for postwar intelligence. The National Security Act of 1947 ultimately codified these decisions, and collectively they set the course of American intelligence for decades to come.

President Truman himself made the first decision. He wanted no repeat of Pearl Harbor. In his view, the Japanese attack might have been prevented "if there had been something like co-ordination of information in the government." There certainly was no such thing in 1941, Truman observed: "In those days the military did not know everything the State Department knew, and the diplomats did not have access to all the Army and Navy knew."[3] Truman could not give the needed coordinating mission to William J. Donovan and his Office of Strategic Services (OSS), which he had disbanded on 1 October 1945. He instead approved a plan that his Joint Chiefs of Staff had proposed for an independent "central" agency to accomplish the "synthesis of departmental intelligence on the strategic and national policy level."[4]

This new intelligence system represented something original in Washington. At its apex would be a capacity for channeling information toward senior civilian and military decision-makers and an analytical function to synthesize "national intelligence" from the mass of data available to the government. A Director of Central Intelligence (DCI) would exercise some significant degree of control over this synthesis. The DCI's position was to be nominally independent of policymaking and hence (at least in theory) a guarantor of the quality of the intelligence reaching the top. The DCI in turn would answer to a committee of Cabinet secretaries to ensure that "no one department could unduly influence the type of intelligence produced," according to the author of this plan, Deputy Chief of Naval Intelligence Sidney Souers. As a White House adviser on intelligence reform, Adm. Souers explained:

---

[1] Harry S. Truman, *Memoirs, Vol. II, Years of Trial and Hope* (Garden City, NY: Doubleday, 1956), 46.
[2] Joint Chiefs of Staff to Secretary of War Henry Stimson and Secretary of the Navy James Forrestal, "Establishment of a Central Intelligence Agency Upon Liquidation of OSS," 19 September 1945, reprinted in Department of State, *Foreign Relations of the United States*, 1945–1950, *Emergence of the Intelligence Establishment* (Washington, DC: Government Printing Office, 1996) [hereinafter cited as FRUS], 41.
[3] Truman, *Years of Trial and Hope*, 56.
[4] Joint Chiefs of Staff to Stimson and Forrestal, "Establishment of a Central Intelligence Agency," FRUS, 41. The Joint Chiefs' proposal had evolved since late 1944, when Gen. William J. Donovan's proposals for a peacetime intelligence establishment had prompted several agencies to think about counter-proposals of their own.

The evaluation of information is not an exact science and every safeguard should be imposed to prevent any one department from having the opportunity to interpret information in such a way as to make it seem to support previously accepted policies or preconceived notions.[5]

By the time Souers penned these words in December 1945, many senior administration officials agreed with his conception of the proposed intelligence agency's role.[6] In essence, Souers held that the President and his key advisers needed a control variable against which to test the intelligence and policy advice coming from the departments. Only a free-standing intelligence agency could provide such a perspective. Objectivity was valued, but independence from departmental views on national security policy was the principal goal.

In January 1946, President Truman appointed Adm. Souers as the first Director of Central Intelligence. As head of a small interdepartmental Central Intelligence Group (CIG), the DCI was to "accomplish the correlation and evaluation of intelligence relating to the national security, and the appropriate dissemination within the Government of the resulting strategic and national policy intelligence."[7] President Truman in effect made Souers his personal intelligence adviser, assigning his

office the responsibility of summarizing the daily flood of cables, memos, reports, and dispatches coming to the White House.

The Truman administration's second major decision, reached soon after the formation of CIG in early 1946, was to find a leader and a home for the clandestine operational capabilities built during the course of the war. Again, it could not be Gen. Donovan or his OSS. When OSS was dissolved the previous autumn, its research and analysis branch was transferred to the Department of State, while the War Department absorbed its surviving operational units, including its clandestine stations abroad. Few people in Washington understood the scope of the secret campaigns launched by OSS and the military, but that handful of officials wanted no repetition of wartime incidents in which the secret activities of one agency jeopardized those of another.[8] To reduce the chance of such conflicts, in September 1945 the Joint Chiefs proposed that the director of a new central agency should further the "coordination of intelligence activities related to the national security."[9]

When President Truman approved the appointment of a DCI, the remnants of the OSS operational branches residing in the War Department lobbied for a transfer to the new Central Intelligence Group. DCI Souers heard their plea, and, by the end of 1946, selected OSS veterans,

---

[5] Sidney Souers to Clark M. Clifford, "Central Intelligence Agency," 27 December 1945, reprinted in FRUS, 157–58.
[6] Secretary of War Robert Patterson argued with State that "intelligence must be divorced from policy making." (Minutes of a 26 December 1945 meeting of the Acting Secretary of State with the Secretaries of War and Navy, reprinted in FRUS, 153.) Forrestal's aides were making a similar case with their Army and State counterparts, saying the director of the new central intelligence agency should "not be identified with any of the departments concerned"; see Mathias F. Correa, special assistant, to Forrestal, 27 December 1945, in ibid., 156.
[7] Harry S. Truman to the Secretary of State, the Secretary of War, and the Secretary of the Navy, 22 January 1946, reprinted in FRUS, 178–79.
[8] A notorious example was OSS' heist of material from the code room of the Japanese Embassy in Lisbon in June 1943. Tokyo instituted new security measures, and allied codebreakers briefly feared they would lose a vital window into Japanese communications. The head of US Army intelligence, Maj. Gen. George Strong, condemned the "ill-advised and amateurish" activities of OSS, calling Donovan's office "a menace to the security of the nation," and Assistant Secretary of War Robert Lovett cited the caper in discussing intelligence reform in November 1945. See Bradley F. Smith, *The Shadow Warriors: OSS and the Origins of the CIA* (New York: Basic Books, 1983), 220–21; and also "Meeting of the Secretaries of State, War, and Navy" [meeting minutes], 14 November 1945, reprinted in FRUS, 110. The Secretaries of State, War, and Navy later explained to Congress that central coordination of intelligence operations was essential because, with "a multitude of espionage agencies," the agents in the field "tend to uncover each other." National Intelligence Authority to Clare Hoffman (R-MI), Chairman, House Committee on Expenditures in the Executive Departments, 26 June 1947, reprinted in FRUS, 311.
[9] Joint Chiefs of Staff to Stimson and Forrestal, "Establishment of a Central Intelligence Agency," 41.

assets, and files had formed the CIG's Office of Special Operations. Although paramilitary and "psychological warfare" elements of OSS had been demobilized by then, CIG nonetheless gained a network of overseas stations and growing espionage, liaison, and counterintelligence skills.[10] Thus the DCI took command of a substantial portion of all US clandestine activities abroad, as well as greater authority to coordinate those activities not under his direct control. The active operational intelligence capability that the United States had developed in the war had found a permanent institutional base.

Most nations do not combine executive intelligence synthesis and operational coordination in one central office of the sort that President Truman authorized in January 1946. The marriage of these two functions in the new CIG was a response to a specific set of historical circumstances in the immediate aftermath of World War II. It might never have happened at all—or not in the same way—at another time. The fact that it did, however, made the DCI the titular head of American intelligence, who was to oversee an intelligence establishment with two main missions: providing strategic warning of threats to the nation and coordinating clandestine activities abroad.

The Truman administration's third key decision was to ensure that American intelligence remained a loose confederation of agencies with no strong direction from either civilian or military decisionmakers. In late 1945, while reviewing intelligence reform proposals, President Truman endorsed the Army and Navy view that "every department required its own intelligence."[11] His January 1946 order that appointed a DCI and established CIG accordingly stipulated that the "existing intelligence agencies…shall continue to collect, evaluate, correlate, and disseminate departmental intelligence."[12] This concession, while necessary to win military and FBI assent to the creation of CIG, soon had unintended consequences. President Truman—and in all likelihood his advisers as well—lacked current knowledge of the true state of "departmental" intelligence. They were unaware, for example, of how far the departmental boundaries that severely limited CIG's ability to conduct investigations within the United States would complicate its counterintelligence work. Moreover, the sprawling but effective military intelligence capabilities built during World War II were being rapidly and inexorably demobilized in 1946, creating a chronic weakness in military intelligence that would last for decades and affect the development of the US Intelligence Community in the Cold War.

The sweeping reform of American intelligence between 1945 and 1947 came about because a determined President who wanted to reshape the national security establishment took full advantage of the opportunity provided him in the wake of the largest war in history. President Truman's initiatives received statutory ratification from Congress in the National Security Act of 1947. Section 102 of this Act, which transformed CIG into the CIA, largely reiterated the missions that Truman had stated in his January 1946 directive. The new Act unified (after a fashion) the armed services, created a Secretary of Defense, an independent Air Force, the CIA, and the National Security Council (NSC). It laid a firm legal and institutional foundation upon which to apply many of the lessons learned in World War II. It is still (with its many amendments) the charter of the US national security establishment.

---

[10] Michael Warner, "Prolonged Suspense: The Fortier Board and the Transformation of the Office of Strategic Services," *Journal of Intelligence History* 2 (June 2002): 74–76.
[11] Truman, *Years of Trial and Hope*, 57.
[12] Truman to the Secretaries of State, War, and Navy, 22 January 1946, 178–179. The directive also included a related provision, that CIG should exercise "no police, law enforcement or internal security functions," nor should it make "investigations inside the continental limits of the United States."

Construction of an Intelligence Community, 1948–53

As the shape of the new Cold War emerged more clearly in 1948, both Congress and the White House commissioned studies of the American intelligence establishment. These parallel studies, the Eberstadt Report and the Dulles Report, were the earliest independent appraisals of American intelligence as a system. The Eberstadt Report reinforced the prescriptions of the more ambitious Dulles Report, which played a major role in shaping the CIA and the Intelligence Community after the outbreak of the Korean War in 1950.

The First Hoover Commission's Eberstadt Report, 1948–49

Just before the passage of the National Security Act in July 1947, the Republican Congress had appointed a commission, chaired by former President Herbert Hoover, to examine the functioning of the Executive Branch. This commission in turn created a task force under Ferdinand Eberstadt, a colleague of the new Secretary of Defense, James Forrestal, to study the national security structure, including intelligence.[1] Eberstadt's panel heard testimony from intelligence officials—particularly the leadership of CIA—in September 1948 and finished its draft late in the year. The Eberstadt task force's published report to Congress concluded: "Intelligence is the first line of defense in the atomic age." By creating the CIA directly under the NSC, the National Security Act had recognized CIA's "preeminent role in defense planning." The report found that CIA had unsatisfactory relationships with several of the individual departmental intelligence services, which had produced "too many disparate intelligence estimates" that were often subjective and biased. Although sound in principle, CIA needed improvement in practice. "It is not now properly organized," the report noted, and the authors recommended vigorous efforts to improve CIA's internal structure and the quality of its product, "especially in the fields of scientific and medical intelligence."[2] While "the basic framework for a sound intelligence organization now exists," the report declared, "[t]hat framework must be fleshed out by proper personnel and sound administrative measures."[3]

The classified section of the Eberstadt Report offered a more extensive examination of the intelligence enterprise. CIA was "the apex of a pyramidal intelligence structure," but it had not met the expectation that it would be the major source of intelligence "on which broad national policy could be soundly based."[4] Personnel represented the main problem for CIA and the other agencies. In the military intelligence arms especially, most of the "skilled and experienced personnel of wartime" had left government service since the war. Those that remained had seen "their organizations and systems ruined by superior officers with no experience, little capacity, and no imagination."[5] Although the task force members were briefed on CIA's newly

The Dulles Report, the national emergency in Korea, and Smith's forceful leadership, helped shape the nation's disparate intelligence agencies into something recognizable as an Intelligence Community.

---

[1] Eberstadt was a former chairman of the Army Munitions Board and former Vice Chairman of the War Production Board who had overseen the production of a report on the question of "unification" of the armed services for Forrestal in the summer of 1945.

[2] The Committee on the National Security Organization, *National Security Organization: A Report with Recommendations*, prepared for the Commission on the Organization of the Executive Branch of the Government, 15 Nov. 1948, 76 and 16 (hereinafter cited as "Unclassified Eberstadt Report"). This unclassified published Eberstadt Report can be found in Executive Registry Job 86B00269R, box 2, folder 1. Congress chartered the larger panel, the Hoover Commission, in July 1947.

[3] The unclassified Eberstadt Report's findings and conclusions were largely based on the more extended classified report drafted by John Bross, an OSS veteran and later a senior CIA official. Ludwell Lee Montague, *General Walter Bedell Smith as Director of Central Intelligence: October 1950—February 1953* (University Park: Pennsylvania State University Press, 1992), 124. This report (hereinafter cited as "Classified Eberstadt Report") formed the chapter, "The Central Intelligence Agency: National and Service Intelligence," in the classified Volume II of the commission's national security organization report. Its pages are numbered 25–60, and the best CIA copy is in Executive Registry Job 86B00269R, box 14, folder 132. For the "framework" quote, see pages 40–41.

[4] "Classified Eberstadt Report," 31–32, 37–38, 44–45, 47, 59–60.

[5] Ibid., 39–40.

authorized covert action capability and were aware of the armed services' signals intelligence programs, the Eberstadt Report said little about operational matters (the classified report was written at the Confidential level, too low in any event to permit discussion of these topics). In short, although the report's authors had spotted weaknesses in military intelligence, they had not probed deeply enough into the problem to understand its causes or propose solutions.

Unique among postwar surveys, the Eberstadt Report projected no organizational change in the Intelligence Community. Change is disruptive in itself, the report declared, and the intelligence services' great present need was for "a relatively reorganization-free period in which to work out their problems." Once action had been taken on those suggested reforms that were accepted, the report concluded, "CIA and other Government intelligence agencies should be permitted a period of internal development free from the disruption of continual examination and as free as possible from publicity." [6]

The NSC's Dulles Report, 1948–49

The Eberstadt Report, completed on 15 November 1948, got little attention when former President Hoover submitted it to a new Democratic Congress on 13 January 1949. It was in any case overshadowed by a long, detailed, and critical survey of the CIA and related intelligence activities prepared for the

The key to an effective intelligence system was for CIA to perform its statutory coordinating role in operations and analysis.

National Security Council (NSC). With a new intelligence system in place in the fall of 1947, NSC officials and DCI Roscoe Hillenkoetter had decided to review the intelligence system's development since the war, to determine how the new NSC should exercise routine oversight of CIA.[7] In early 1948 the NSC asked three intelligence veterans—Allen Dulles, William Jackson, and Matthias Correa—to report on the Agency. The team submitted its report to the NSC on 1 January 1949.[8] Although focused on the CIA, the team had also received NSC permission to examine (as had the Eberstadt Report) "such intelligence activities of other Government Departments and Agencies as relate to the national security, in order to make recommendations for their effective operation and overall coordination." [9]

Dulles, Jackson, and Correa began from the insight that World War II had changed everything. Modern crises could be catastrophic: America was vulnerable to a "sudden and possibly devastating attack." Compounding this peril were the tactics of potential adversaries. An "iron curtain" now veiled the workings of regimes from the Elbe to the Yangtze. Far-flung communist fifth-column activities both in the United States and abroad presented a new kind of threat to American security. Moreover, with the advent of the atomic bomb, science had opened an entirely new field that, while vital for US defense, also posed new problems for intelligence collection and coordination. As the first line of defense, intelligence had to be

---

[6] Ibid., 48, 59–60.

[7] Arthur B. Darling, *The Central Intelligence Agency: An Instrument of Government, to 1950* (University Park: Pennsylvania State University Press, 1990), 299. Also see Montague, 39–40.

[8] Dulles had won fame after the war when his exploits as OSS chief of station in Bern, Switzerland, emerged. Widely recognized as a leading civilian expert on intelligence, he had testified on the proposed National Security Act in 1947. Matthias F. Correa, a former New York District Attorney, had worked in OSS counterintelligence in Italy before becoming an aide to Secretary of the Navy James Forrestal dealing with intelligence reform in 1945. William H. Jackson, a New York lawyer and banker, who had been the Assistant Military Attaché for Air in London and Chief of the Secret Intelligence Branch, G-2, European Theater, in World War II, became DDCI in 1950.

[9] The formal citation for the Dulles Report is: Intelligence Report Group, "The Central Intelligence Organization and National Organization for Intelligence," 1 January 1949, iv. It will be cited hereinafter as the Dulles Report. The Summary of the Dulles Report is reprinted in FRUS; see in particular page 903. Also see Darling, 302. To assist the authors in their task, the NSC on 13 January 1948 had authorized and directed the DCI and the departmental intelligence chiefs to give the team "access to all information and facilities required for their survey, except details concerning intelligence sources and methods." "National Security Council Resolution," 13 January 1948, reprinted in FRUS, 827.

a full-time pursuit, not just a wartime activity. It had both to warn of threats and to prepare to serve effectively in a conflict. America and its leaders, the Dulles Report contended, had overcome their suspicions of secret government and had tried to strike a balance between freedom of the press and the need "for silence on certain phases of intelligence."[10]

The Dulles Report echoed several Eberstadt Report conclusions. The authors found that the National Security Act of 1947 had provided "a framework upon which a sound intelligence system can be built," and that to accomplish its vital coordinating mission CIA had been "properly placed under the National Security Council."[11] But CIA had not yet effectively carried out its vital role of coordinating intelligence activities and judgments relating to the national security.[12] Building an efficient intelligence structure would take time and would require the patient provision of "competent and highly trained men and women."[13]

The Dulles Report's authors were able to delve deeper than the Eberstadt Report into CIA's situation and relationship with other intelligence activities. CIA's creation (as "a semi-autonomous highly centralized agency with a broad variety of intelligence responsibilities") marked a departure from the general pattern that other countries had followed. Such a degree of centralization entailed certain disadvantages, the report conceded, but it could "be justified, provided that [CIA's] distinctive functions…are handled according to their special requirements."[14]

The key to an effective intelligence system was for CIA to perform its statutory coordinating role in operations and analysis. A properly functioning CIA "should be able more effectively to carry out the duties assigned to it by law and thus bring our over-all intelligence system closer to that point of efficiency which the national security demands."[15] The Agency should operate on clear principles:

Unless the Central Intelligence Agency performs an essential service for each of [the] departments and coordinates their intelligence activities, it will fail in its mission. The Central Intelligence Agency should not be merely another intelligence agency duplicating and rivalling [sic] the existing agencies of State, Army, Navy, and Air Force. It should not be a competitor of these agencies, but a contributor to them and should help to coordinate their intelligence activities. It must make maximum use of the resources of existing agencies; it must not duplicate their work but help to put an end to existing duplication by seeing to it that the best qualified agency in each phase of the intelligence field should assume and carry out its particular responsibility.[16]

Unfortunately, the report continued, the Agency was not operating along these lines:

The principal defect of the Central Intelligence Agency is that its direction, administrative organization and performance do not show sufficient appreciation of the Agency's assigned functions, particularly in the fields of intelligence coordination and the production of intelligence estimates. The result has been that the Central Intelligence Agency has tended to

---

[10] Ibid., 15–18
[11] Ibid., 1–5, see also 22–23.
[12] Ibid., 2–5.
[13] Ibid., 16–17, 147.
[14] Ibid., 23.
[15] Ibid., 14.
[16] Ibid., 26–27.

become just one more intelligence agency producing intelligence in competition with older established agencies of the Government departments.[17]

Here the Dulles Report implicitly differed from the Eberstadt Report, which had subtly suggested that the NSC needed to start providing positive guidance to CIA. In their report, Dulles, Jackson, and Correa conceded that decisionmakers needed to do a better job of communicating their needs to intelligence:

It is, indeed, a fundamental failing of the American intelligence services that, in general, they are not advised of the current needs of policy-makers. Unfortunately, continuing effort is rarely made by intelligence consumers to guide intelligence activities toward the most meaningful targets.[18]

This problem notwithstanding, the Dulles Report suggested that the CIA was the weak link in the system, and that its weakness was the result not of a lack of authorities but of "inadequacies of direction" from the current Director of Central Intelligence, Roscoe Hillenkoetter.[19] An effective DCI, the report declared, would have to

show a much greater concern than hitherto with the general problem of coordination of intelligence activities[,] which is one of his essential statutory duties. His is a responsibility to all of the departments concerned with national security; it can be properly discharged by leadership, imagination, initiative and a realization that only a joining of efforts can achieve the desired results.[20]

While acknowledging that a measure of CIA's and the DCI's difficulties resulted from the older intelligence agencies' "suspicion and distrust," the Dulles Report nonetheless insisted that "what is needed today is for the Central Intelligence Agency to prove that it can and will carry out its assigned duties."[21]

Among the assigned duties that the Dulles Report found CIA had neglected was the production of "national intelligence," especially in the preparation of national intelligence estimates. The original CIG, the report explained, had envisioned a small organization limited strictly to national intelligence problems, which would base its work primarily on other departments' reports and estimates rather than employ a large research and analysis organization of its own. The changed character of this organization and diffusion of its duties, however, had made its output of national intelligence now unimpressive. CIA had become "an independent producer of national intelligence, the quality of whose product is variable and the influence of which is questionable."[22] To remedy this, the report proposed the creation of an Estimates Division, "a small group of highly selected individuals whose task it would be to draw upon and review the specialized intelligence product of the departmental agencies in order to prepare…a finished national intelligence estimate." Moreover, to make them the most authoritative estimates available to policymakers, all of the principal intelligence agencies were to participate in and approve them. This was one of the Dulles Report's most significant recommendations, which Lt. Gen. Walter Bedell Smith promptly implemented by forming the Office and Board of National Estimates when he took office as DCI in October 1950.[23]

---

17 Ibid., 11.
18 Ibid., 127.
19 Ibid., 11.
20 Ibid., 60.
21 Ibid., 163.
22 Ibid., 72.
23 Ibid., 76–82, "Proposals for Improving the Production of National Estimates."

The Dulles Report also offered some insightful suggestions for ensuring tighter coordination between communications intelligence, operations, and diplomacy. Its authors were prohibited, however, from looking too closely at the functioning of the cryptologic services. The National Security Council did not allow the Dulles team to critique "departmental intelligence operations…in the collection of communications intelligence."[24] The report's authors thus found themselves unable "to express a judgment upon the efficiency of the present arrangements for the production of communications intelligence through the separate establishments of the Army and the Navy."[25]

The Dulles Report did a more thorough job with human intelligence, a field its authors knew well. The authors noted that since communist countries offered little open source information, the United States was forced to rely more on clandestine means.[26] Although satisfied with the early progress of CIA's clandestine collection office, they offered several constructive suggestions.[27] The report also called for better management of counterintelligence activities, both within CIA and across the intelligence system, noting "the danger of foreign espionage and the menace of fifth-column activities does not stop or start at our national boundaries." The Agency had not yet "adequately exploited" counterintelligence

> as a source of positive intelligence information, as a channel for deception, as a means of protecting espionage operations and as a basis for penetrating fifth-column operations abroad, which may be tied in with fifth-column operations here.[28]

The CIA and FBI had to maintain closer relations with each other. The NSC and CIA had to take the initiative in this field, both in inviting the Bureau to sit on interagency advisory bodies and in crafting and implementing firmer directives that would enable the Agency to serve the purpose set forth in the National Security Act, "of coordinating those phases of domestic intelligence and counter-intelligence which relate to the national security."[29]

The Dulles Report and DCI Smith's Reforms, 1950–53

The Dulles Report was one of the most influential outside evaluations in the history of the Intelligence Community. It owed its success in no small portion to its authors' understanding that Congress and the White House had intended the Central Intelligence Agency to coordinate both operations and analysis—that the definition of "intelligence" in its title had to include both activities. The Dulles Report added to the sentiment in the Truman administration that the CIA needed stronger leadership. Although the NSC soon endorsed many of the Dulles Report's recommendations, the question of replacing DCI Hillenkoetter became entangled in administration debates over the direction of defense policy. The reforms that the NSC had mandated were largely held in abeyance until June 1950, when the CIA's failure to foresee the sudden North Korean invasion of South Korea spurred President Truman to appoint a new DCI, Lt. Gen. Walter Bedell Smith, USA. 'Beetle' Smith, who had been Gen. Dwight Eisenhower's chief of staff in Europe and Truman's ambassador to the Soviet Union, took office as DCI on 7 October 1950, with the determination and mandate

The Dulles Report was one of the most influential outside evaluations in the history of the Intelligence Community.

---

[24] Ibid., iv.
[25] Ibid., 59; also cf 126.
[26] Ibid., 108.
[27] Ibid., cf 119 and 128.
[28] Ibid., 125.
[29] Ibid., 56–58, 125–126, and 144–145.

to reshape the organization and make US intelligence work as a team.[30]

In November 1950, within weeks of Smith's arrival, America suffered one of its worst battlefield defeats when Chinese troops fell upon Gen. Douglas MacArthur's overstretched forces in North Korea. Disaster was averted and the front stabilized by January 1951, but the debacle marked the second major US intelligence warning failure in six months. Neither the CIA nor any other US intelligence body foresaw the size or effectiveness of communist China's sudden massive intervention in the war. This lapse brought home the urgency of the new DCI's reforms.

Smith had gone to work with a will, hiring William Jackson as his Deputy Director of Central Intelligence (DDCI) and Allen Dulles as deputy director for operations. Working rapidly along the lines proposed in the Dulles Report, Smith, Jackson and Dulles tightened CIA's internal administration, reformed its production of finished intelligence, and established a clear division of labor among the various components of the Intelligence Community.

Smith followed the NSC's blueprint to reform what he considered one of CIA's main weaknesses, its office for analyzing and disseminating intelligence. Under Smith's predecessors, Agency products represented the judgments of CIA analysts but had not always reflected the views and information of other intelligence agencies. Smith had been angered to discover on arriving that CIA's Office of Reports and Estimates (ORE) had no current, coordinated estimate of the Korean situation. He soon broke ORE into three pieces.[31] To make CIA the producer of "the most authoritative esti-

mates available to policy makers," the first of the three new units comprised a board of experts and staff to draft and coordinate national intelligence estimates—the Board and Office of National Estimates. In addition, Smith formed a new "current intelligence" office to produce the daily bulletin for the President, and a research office to conduct analyses that were beyond the scope of the established intelligence services. The success of Smith's reforms depended upon departmental intelligence from other agencies. The members of the Intelligence Community were to perform the basic analysis of subjects in their designated fields, while CIA would cease duplicating their efforts and focus on integrating the whole effort of American intelligence analysis.

The improvement of departmental intelligence that Smith desired also made progress during his tenure as DCI. The armed services had continued to maintain separate cryptologic efforts under a loose confederation called the Armed Forces Security Agency, which reported to the Joint Chiefs of Staff. Complaints about signals intelligence support for the Korean effort provoked Smith's anger, however, and at his urging the National Security Council in 1952 replaced this system with a new National Security Agency (NSA), subordinated to the Secretary of Defense.[32] The change preserved the cryptologic arms of the various services but recognized the "national" importance of their collective effort to provide tighter coordination and better support for the Secretary of Defense.

DCI Smith's major contribution to the emergence of the Intelligence Community was that, for the first time, he realized and used the DCI's latent authority to lead the intelligence estab-

[30] Truman nominated and the Senate confirmed Smith as DCI in late August 1950, but major surgery prevented his taking office until 7 October. When informed of his appointment, Smith told a friend, "I expect the worst and I am sure I won't be disappointed." D. K. R. Crosswell, *The Chief of Staff: The Military Career of General Walter Bedell Smith* (New York: Greenwood, 1991), 122 and 332. Montague, 55–56.
[31] Montague, 151.
[32] Montague, 253–54. See also David A. Hatch and Robert Louis Benson, "The Korean War: The SIGINT Background," National Security Agency Center for Cryptologic History, 2000, 15–16.

lishment. Not everything turned out as he envisioned, but by the time he stepped down in early 1953, he had consolidated CIA's major functions, recast its place in the overall intelligence structure, and set clear missions and roles for the departmental elements of that system. The Department of State and Joint Chiefs of Staff yielded their remaining operational roles to the CIA and the Secretary of Defense.[33] At the same time, Smith's reforms sought to keep the services and departments strong in intelligence analysis—an arrangement that would not work out so well (and would eventually prompt calls for new investigations of intelligence). The combination of the Dulles Report's blueprint, the national emergency in Korea, and Smith's forceful leadership, had thus helped shape the nation's disparate intelligence agencies into something recognizable as an Intelligence Community.[34]

---

[33] For more on State and JCS in the direction of operations, see Montague, 206–208; as well as Mark Stout, "The Pond: Running Agents for State, War, and the CIA," *Studies in Intelligence* 48, no. 3 (2004), 77–78.
[34] Indeed, the term "Intelligence Community" first began to appear in descriptions of the US intelligence system in 1952, toward the end of Gen. Smith's tenure as DCI. Montague, 74.

The Collection Revolution, 1954–60

The decade ending in 1960 saw two principal studies advocating further adjustments in the Intelligence Community, as it exploited new technological means of collecting data and the White House concentrated its powers to run the Cold War. The first study was commissioned by Congress and led by Gen. Mark Clark, USA (Ret). Although it identified a number of problem areas—such as the Intelligence Community's management and accountability to Congress—its actual results were minimal. Indeed, before the congressional investigations of the mid-1970s, studies sponsored by Congress had very limited influence on the structure or work of CIA and the Intelligence Community. The second study, commissioned by President Eisenhower and led by CIA Inspector General Lyman Kirkpatrick, was more tightly focused than Gen. Clark's and (as might be expected from its presidential sponsorship) produced significant results.

The Second Hoover Commission's Clark Report, 1955

By the time the Republicans recaptured Congress and the White House in 1953, the issue of collection was becoming vital. When the new Congress gave a resurrected Hoover Commission another charter to examine the Executive Branch, the commission created another intelligence task force, under Gen. Mark Clark, to study and make recommendations on all intelligence activities of the Federal government.[1] Clark's panel began its work in October 1954 and first met early the next month. In May 1955 it submitted two reports: one Top Secret (with lengthy annexes) for the President, and another unclassified for the Hoover Commission and Congress.[2]

The Clark task force adopted assumptions concerning US national security similar to those of the Eberstadt and Dulles inquiries. Over the last generation Americans had had to set aside their once secure indifference to foreign affairs: "Technological developments and political realignments in modern times" had compelled American vigilance and action in the larger world. The United States had emerged from World War II as the greatest military power and the leader of the free world. The demands of global leadership and the advent of atomic bombs had now "intensified the need for adequate and timely intelligence so that we might fulfill our responsibilities in international affairs and ensure our own survival."[3]

The Clark report's results were to some extent predetermined by President Eisenhower's reluctance to let the panel examine CIA's clandestine operations. When the Hoover Commission named Mark Clark to investigate intelligence, the President asked the famous aviator, Lt. Gen. James H. Doolittle, USAFR, and a panel of consultants to undertake a quick study of CIA's covert activities. To ensure that these matters remained outside the Clark task force's purview, Eisenhower told Doolittle to confer with Clark "in order to avoid any unnecessary duplication of work."[4]

---

[1] Congress in July 1953 chartered the second Commission on Organization of the Executive Branch of the Government, which Herbert Hoover again chaired. The Hoover Commission's final report was due on 31 May 1955, when the commission would go out of existence. Members of the Clark Task Force were Adm. Richard L. Conolly, USN (Ret), a former Deputy Chief of Naval Operations; Ernest F. Hollings, the speaker pro tempore of South Carolina's House of Representatives; California businessman Henry Kearns; Edward V. Rickenbacker, World War I flying ace and president of Eastern Air Lines; and Donald S. Russell, a former Assistant Secretary of State. The staff director was Maj. Gen. James G. Christiansen, USA (Ret).

[2] The unclassified report to Congress used much of the classified version's text. Unless otherwise noted, this section cites the unclassified version.

[3] Clark Report, 11–12.

[4] Gen. Doolittle and his team submitted their report, "Covert Activities of the Central Intelligence Agency," on 30 September 1954, just as the Clark task force was starting its work. The quotation comes from President Eisenhower's letter to James H. Doolittle, 26 July 1954, reprinted as Appendix A of the Doolittle Report, which has been declassified and released as CIA MORI document 627859.

President Eisenhower's constraint perhaps explains why the Clark report, after struggling to define intelligence, arrived at the following: "Intelligence deals with all the things which should be known in advance of initiating a course of action." This definition allowed the Clark report to sidestep secret activities not directly tied to the collection of intelligence. Nevertheless, intelligence as information for decisionmaking was still too broad a definition, for the task force had no writ or desire to comment on the overall management of information in the Executive Branch. It thus felt obliged to limit its inquiry to "foreign" intelligence, in which the adjective denoted "the target of information as distinct from the geographical source."[5]

This clarification still left the task force with a "Herculean job" and the prospect of providing only sketchy results in the time allotted. The Clark task force seemed to feel that "the Intelligence Community"—its term for "the machinery for accomplishing our intelligence objectives"—was getting too complicated to understand. There were at least a dozen departments and agencies "engaged in intelligence in one form or another," with another 10 or so involved in minor ways.[6] Faced with this profusion, the classified version of the Clark report hinted that the task force had thrown up its collective hands and rather arbitrarily narrowed its inquiry to "the departments and agencies whose entire or primary responsibilities lie in the field of positive foreign intelligence as it pertains to national defense and security, and in whose care vast amounts of money and unique authority have been entrusted."[7]

These definitions and limitations meant that the Clark task force would not really judge the quality of intelligence support to foreign policy, either in improving decisionmaking or in executing policies. Instead, the Clark report confined itself largely to issues of management: how well the CIA and the Intelligence Community seemed to function and interact, and how those functions and interactions could be improved through leadership and oversight.

The Clark report praised Allen Dulles—now serving as DCI—as "industrious, objective, selfless, enthusiastic, and imaginative." The report's authors nevertheless worried that in his enthusiasm Dulles had "taken upon himself too many burdensome duties and responsibilities on the operational side of CIA's activities." The report cautioned, "The glamour and excitement of some angles of our intelligence effort must not be permitted to overshadow other vital phases of the work or to cause neglect of primary functions." Moreover, CIA needed to correct certain administrative flaws that had developed in it.[8]

Deeply concerned over the lack of adequate intelligence data from behind the Iron Curtain, the authors of the Clark report called for "greater concentration on the collection of intelligence information from our primary target[s]—Russia and her satellites, and Communist China."[9] This criticism of collection on key intelligence problems marked a turning point for surveys of the Intelligence Community. Hitherto such reports had stressed procedural problems and reforms, and had not focused on the quantity or sources of data collected. Henceforth they would scrutinize what was collected as well as the entities that collected it.

What was to be done? The Clark report seemed to suggest that the remedy was both

---

[5] Ibid., 18, 26.
[6] Ibid., 13, 17–18.
[7] Ibid., xi, classified version.
[8] The task force also declared: "We discovered no valid ground for the suspicion that the CIA or any other element of the intelligence family was being effectively contaminated by any organized subversive or communistic clique." Ibid., 13–14.
[9] Ibid., 14.

organizational and technological. At CIA, reorganization was needed to ensure that each of its functions "gets adequate attention without diversionary interest."[10] The larger problem of collection against the communist powers demanded "greater boldness at the policy level, a willingness to accept certain calculated political and diplomatic risks, and full use of technological capabilities." Immediately after this statement, the task force suggested that DCI Dulles needed to spend less time managing CIA and devote more attention to the "broad, overall direction of the Agency and the coordination of the entire intelligence effort." In particular, the DCI should employ "an Executive Director, or 'chief of staff,' of the Agency" so that he might be relieved of "the chore of many day-to-day administrative and operational problems."[11]

The task force also expressed concern "over the absence of satisfactory machinery for the surveillance of the stewardship of the Central Intelligence Agency." This need for closer oversight prompted perhaps the most influential Clark task force suggestion: a "small, permanent commission" comprising "a bipartisan group including members of both Houses of Congress and distinguished private citizens appointed by the President." The full Hoover Commission liked the idea but rejected the proposal for a hybrid private-congressional committee. It urged instead that the President appoint a distinguished private panel and suggested that Congress consider establishing its own joint committee on intelligence.[12] The latter idea foundered amid competing congressional committee jurisdictions, but the former found a receptive audience at the White House.

The Clark Task Force strengthened its case for a new watchdog panel through candid comments in the classified version of its report. It noted that Congress and the White House had created CIA to be "a new agency unique and in many ways strange to our democratic form of government." The Agency "operates without the customary legislative restraints and reins under which other departments must function. Its work is veiled in secrecy, and it is virtually a law unto itself." Secrecy made it difficult to judge how well the Intelligence Community functioned. Indeed, CIA's cumbersome and time-consuming security restrictions had "seriously interfered" with the task force's survey of the Agency's activities. Moreover, the Intelligence Community itself did not know how much it spent. "Precise figures on the cost in money and manpower engaged in intelligence activities…are not a matter of record," and the task force could only guess at the total. "Any attempt to compile such data would require the expenditure of money out of all proportion to the value of the findings."[13]

President Eisenhower soon appointed a panel of wise men, called the President's Board of Consultants for Foreign Intelligence Activities (PBCFIA). Although hardly the "machinery for surveillance" of CIA that the Clark report had recommended, the new board offered the President a source of experienced opinion and advice for improving CIA and the Intelligence Community. This was perhaps the only lasting result of the Clark report, which Congress, having returned to Democratic control in 1955, generally ignored.

The Kirkpatrick Joint Study Group, 1960

Just after the May 1960 U-2 shoot down, President Eisenhower authorized a survey of the Intelligence Community, tasking an ad hoc team of senior intelligence officials from State,

The study led by CIA Inspector General Lyman Kirkpatrick in 1960 was tightly focused and produced significant results.

---

[10] Ibid., 14.

[11] Ibid., 69.

[12] Clark Report, 1–2, 14–15 and 61.

[13] Classified Clark Report, vi, viii, xvii, and xix.

Defense, and CIA. This "Joint Study Group," headed by CIA's respected Inspector General, Lyman B. Kirkpatrick, Jr., worked efficiently to meet a tight deadline. Eisenhower wanted recommendations that he could act upon during his last month in office, which gave the group barely seven months to complete its report. Like the Clark Task Force, moreover, the Joint Study Group concentrated on the informational side of the intelligence business and did not report on covert action or related clandestine activities in support of US foreign policy.[14] Indeed, the team's terms of reference, which the members' principals approved in mid-July, delimited the scope of the group's inquiry to "the organizational and management aspects of the foreign intelligence community."[15]

The final report of the Joint Study Group reflected both the authors' intimate knowledge and their remarkable candor in appraising the strengths and weaknesses of their own home agencies and of the intelligence system itself. Where previous inquiries had only begun to notice the Intelligence Community's main Cold War problem—its inability to collect key information on the Soviet Union—the Joint Study Group faced this issue forthrightly. The two roots of the problem were the Cold War itself and the pace of technological change. Prolonged Soviet-American tension—"[t]he continued threat from an implacable and powerful enemy"—had forced the United States to sustain its intelligence effort "at close to wartime intensity." Decisionmakers needed "the best possible flow of information" about Soviet intentions and capabilities, but were not getting it despite the labors of the Intelligence Community:

> *It cannot be said with any assurance, short of the actual event, that this flow of information is now sufficient to provide the desirable warning and security of command, or assuming that it is now sufficient, that it will not suddenly dry up sometime in the future.*[16]

Technological change was further complicating the situation, producing new weapons and consequent dangers, along with collection opportunities and risks—and vast new expenses. Unfortunately, the agencies themselves were addressing new problems piecemeal instead of attacking them together in an integrated fashion.[17] The intelligence system, the report counseled, "must be a community effort in fact as well as name."[18]

The answer was not a quick organizational fix but a patient campaign to improve coordination. The majority of the Joint Study Group opposed the idea of detaching the DCI from the CIA so that he could concentrate on community affairs, fearing that he would become a mere figurehead if he lost the influence conferred by his ability to command an operating intelligence agency. The DCI instead needed a permanent staff drawn from across the community and devoted solely to community management and coordination issues.[19] In

---

[14] This approach was in keeping with Kirkpatrick's stated preference for defining intelligence as "a compilation and distillation of the total knowledge on any given area or subject." Lyman B. Kirkpatrick, Jr., *The US Intelligence Community: Foreign Policy and Domestic Activities* (Boulder, CO: Westview, 1985 [1973]), 3.

[15] Joint Study Group, "Report on Foreign Intelligence Activities of the United States Government," 15 December 1960, Executive Registry Job 86B00269R, box 2, f. 6. The members were Lyman B. Kirkpatrick, Jr., the chairman and representative of the DCI; Allan Evans, representing the Secretary of State; Gen. Graves B. Erskine, USMC (Ret), representing the Secretary of Defense; Robert M. Macy, representing the director of the Bureau of the Budget; and James S. Lay, Jr., representing the special assistant for national security affairs and the National Security Council. Assisting the group were J. Patrick Coyne of the PBCFIA staff and Jesmond Balmer, the assistant to the DCI for interagency coordination. Kirkpatrick describes the genesis and work of the Joint Study Group in *The Real CIA* (New York: Macmillan, 1968), 206–207, and 215–232.)

[16] Joint Study Group, "Report on Foreign Intelligence Activities," 26–27.

[17] Ibid., 19–21, 129–132.

[18] Ibid., 23.

[19] Ibid., 89–94, 103, 109–110. The group's Defense Department representative dissented from this conclusion.

addition, the United States Intelligence Board—the advisory body charged with coordinating community estimates and requirements—needed to streamline its own work (especially its cumbersome committee structure) and tailor the community's voluminous list of intelligence questions to existing collection capabilities.[20]

Similarly, the Joint Study Group was the first survey to probe the Defense Department's role and performance in the Intelligence Community. Its final report noted that defense intelligence needed a greater exercise of managerial and budgetary powers by the Office of the Secretary, the Joint Chiefs of Staff, and the Director of the National Security Agency. These combined efforts could measurably improve DoD intelligence and thus help integrate and streamline the entire national intelligence system.[21]

The Joint Study Group's report is perhaps principally remembered today for recognizing the weakness of defense intelligence and for advocating several steps towards strengthening intelligence for commanders and decisionmakers. For example, it helped persuade the incoming Kennedy administration to create the Defense Intelligence Agency (DIA). The group's report had not actually called for a new intelligence office under the Secretary of Defense, but rather recommended a modest centralization and insisted that the services should retain their separate organizations.[22] Nevertheless, Secretary of Defense Robert McNamara added some ideas of his own to the report's suggestions, and DIA began operating on 1 October 1961. The individual services' intelligence organizations continued to function, but they lost some of their autonomy and resources to DIA, the Secretary of Defense's own intelligence service. The Joint Study Group, however, could claim paternity for the creation of the National Photographic Intelligence Center (NPIC), the joint CIA-Defense imagery analysis office. Following the group's recommendation, President Eisenhower authorized the new center shortly before leaving office in January 1961.

[20] Ibid., 85–86.
[21] Ibid., 23, 28, 32.
[22] Ibid., 23.

The Schlesinger Report, 1971

The 1960s saw rapid technological innovation and steeply rising costs for both military systems and intelligence collection. The use of satellites and computers for intelligence work brought new capabilities and drove organizational changes. By 1969, the incoming Nixon administration, glimpsing new challenges and opportunities for America in both fields, wondered why the Intelligence Community seemed so ambivalent in supporting White House initiatives. National Security Adviser Henry Kissinger perceived an institutional predisposition toward pessimism and naysaying among the analysts and their managers. President Nixon complained that CIA was infected with political biases and would not give him information on its past activities. Flawed analyses of events in Indochina further annoyed the White House: "What the hell do those clowns do out there in Langley?" the President asked after Washington was surprised by the 1970 coup in Cambodia.[1]

The Nixon administration authorized its own survey of the Intelligence Community in late 1970. The job fell to James Schlesinger, Assistant Director of the White House Office of Management and Budget, who worked closely with Kissinger's NSC staff on the project. Their March 1971 report described a community adapting haphazardly to technological change, and recommended reforms that would eventually prove far reaching.[2]

As might be expected with a budget official in charge of the survey, the resulting report took a hard look at resources. The Schlesinger Report noted two "disturbing phenomena" in the Intelligence Community. The cost of intelligence had exploded over the last decade with "spectacular increases in collection activities." At the same time, however, the community had failed to achieve "a commensurate improvement in the scope and overall quantity of intelligence products." Improved collection technologies—satellite photography, telemetry, and electronic intelligence—had cast doubt on the once-clear lines between "national" and "tactical" intelligence. Uncertain of their missions, the intelligence agencies and armed services had expanded into costly and duplicative ventures while clinging to obsolescent collection systems.[3]

In addition, the vast new quantities of data had outstripped the community's ability—or willingness—to analyze them.[4] Analysts were not exploiting the "richness" of the new data. They had shown little initiative in offering explanations for foreign actions, and had demonstrated a "propensity to overlook...unpleasant possibilities." The expense and impetus of technological developments thus had the perverse effect of worsening this problem, making the collectors more influential in their agencies than the analysts, so that collection guided production instead of vice versa. Consumers also tended to treat intelligence as "a free good, so that demand exceeds supply, priorities are not established, the system becomes overloaded, and the quality of the output suffers."[5] The community's indiscipline and inertia could not be remedied without "a fundamental reform of [its] decisionmaking bodies and procedures."[6] Indeed, since new systems under development were making intelligence even more expensive, and since the President had no real hope of improving the community's performance as it was presently constituted, one

---

[1] Richard Nixon, *RN: The Memoirs of Richard Nixon*, Volume 1 (New York: Warner, 1979 [1978]), 553, 638. Henry Kissinger, *White House Years* (Boston: Little, Brown, 1979), 11, 36, 1180–1181.

[2] James R. Schlesinger, Assistant Director, Office of Management and Budget, "A Review of the Intelligence Community," 10 March 1971, (the original is still classified). The report was drafted by Arnold Donohue of OMB. Hereinafter cited as the Schlesinger Report.

[3] Ibid., 4–6 and 8–9.

[4] Ibid., 1–2.

[5] Ibid., 10–12.

[6] Ibid., 1–2.

might "reasonably argue that, for current performance, he should at least obtain the benefit of lower costs."[7]

The Schlesinger Report recommended a strong dose of management. It presented its advice as a range of options, listing potential advantages and drawbacks for each, and the options it tabled ranged from mild to radical degrees of centralization. The National Security Act of 1947 had granted the DCI authorities deemed sufficient to remedy the "defects in central processing, production, and dissemination" that had hampered the government before Pearl Harbor. The Act had not, however, anticipated the need to "plan and rationalize" the collection of intelligence or to evaluate the quality of its product.[8] Someone had to manage all of these fields, both within the Defense Department and across the community as a whole. The report noted that the required Intelligence Community leader could be anything from a new coordinator in the White House to a full-fledged director of national intelligence, controlling the budgets and personnel of the entire community.

The report offered a similar range of possibilities for a manager of defense intelligence functions, declaring, "changes within the Department of Defense alone could improve the allocation and management of resources and reduce the overall size of the intelligence budget." The Department of Defense had never had an office to exercise "formal responsibility" over defense intelligence. There were two possible ways of devising such a position: a "Director of Defense Intelligence" with broad authorities to exercise on behalf of the secretary (but who would still be responsive to the Intelligence Community's leader); or an Assistant Secretary of Defense for Intelligence to be the secretary's principal staff assistant.[9]

The Schlesinger Report resulted in the appointment of a deputy to the DCI for community affairs and an Assistant Secretary of Defense for Intelligence.

Acting on the Report's Recommendations

The Schlesinger Report's more radical options would have required new legislation and were controversial even within the Nixon administration, but some of its milder options were nevertheless fully or partially implemented. These resulted in the appointment of a deputy to the DCI for community affairs and of an Assistant Secretary of Defense for Intelligence, the merger of the service cryptologic organizations in a Central Security Service under the National Security Agency, and the creation of the Defense Mapping Agency and an Intelligence Community Staff to support the DCI. Since the turmoil of Watergate and the congressional investigations of the mid-1970s blunted the impact of President Nixon's augmentation of the DCI's powers, the implementation of these milder options was the Schlesinger Report's most lasting legacy. Indeed, every DCI since the presidential decision of November 1971 was expected to oversee the preparation of the Intelligence Community's budgets, to establish intelligence requirements and priorities, and to ensure the quality of community products.

Before the Nixon administration could fully implement its vision of a new Intelligence Community, controversy over ending the Vietnam War and the Watergate scandal in the White House distracted policymakers and intelligence officials. The Cold War consensus that had held since the Truman administration was eroding by the early 1970s, and responsible voices in Washington began questioning the legitimacy of two staples of postwar American foreign policy: military intervention in overseas conflicts, and the use of covert action against communists and their allies. Congressional critics used their subpoena power to investigate Nixon administration wrongdoing and credi-

---

[7] Ibid., 40 and 44–45.
[8] Ibid., 13–14.
[9] Ibid., 34–38.

ble allegations of serious intelligence misconduct, including infringements upon civil liberties. The Watergate investigations of 1973 that brought about President Nixon's resignation were followed in less than two years by the Rockefeller, Church, and Pike inquiries into the CIA and the Intelligence Community. By mid-decade, President Gerald Ford and his intelligence advisers, beleaguered by criticism, worried that Congress might overreact by mandating sweeping and counterproductive reforms.

Three Studies in 1975

The Murphy, Taylor, and Ogilivie Reports contributed to the administration's response to congressional investigations and led to follow-up on the Schlesinger Report's recommendations.

As Congress pressed forward with special House and Senate committee investigations of intelligence abuses and performance, three more studies—one from Congress and two from the executive branch—were undertaken and completed. None had the heft of the Schlesinger Report or of earlier surveys, and all three were overshadowed by the better-known congressional investigations. The first, the Murphy Commission Report of June 1975, treated intelligence only in passing, as a piece of the larger American foreign policy establishment. The second, the October 1975 Taylor Report, lacked persuasiveness partly because CIA produced it on its own at the request of its besieged DCI, William Colby. The third, the November 1975 Ogilvie Report, was drafted in the White House so quickly that its authors had little time to study the complexities of American intelligence. These reports' assessments and conclusions nevertheless modestly influenced the continuing evolution of the Intelligence Community.

The Murphy Commission, June 1975

Congress in July 1972 had authorized a study commission to recommend improvements in the organization and procedures of the government for conducting foreign policy. This blue-ribbon panel, led by retired Deputy Secretary of State Robert Murphy, included members of Congress along with distinguished citizens appointed by the White House. In this it was not unlike the 1947 and 1953 Hoover Commission panels that had examined intelligence years earlier. It began slowly, had its term extended a year, and did not finish until June 1975.[1] The report's brief chapter on intelligence defended it as essential to national security and effective foreign policy, and noted "considerable progress" in recent years in improving analysis, controlling costs, and raising professional standards of conduct. Nevertheless, various management changes were needed to provide "firmer direction and oversight."[2]

The main remedy proposed was tighter presidential and congressional supervision. Since it was "neither possible nor desirable to give the DCI line authority" over the entire Intelligence Community, he would need a closer relationship with the President if he was to guide the community's affairs. The DCI should move his desk closer to the White House and enjoy "direct access" to the Oval Office, while delegating day-to-day supervision of CIA to his deputy. As a symbol of this change, the Agency itself would be renamed the Foreign Intelligence Agency, and the DCI would become the Director of Foreign Intelligence. The President's Foreign Intelligence Advisory Board (a revived version of Eisenhower's PBCFIA) should also gain more access to the President, a bigger staff, and a stronger role in evaluating community performance as a whole. Covert action should have tighter NSC control. Finally, Congress should create a select, joint committee on "national security" to review and coordinate oversight of foreign and national security policies; the committee would supplement, not replace, the existing foreign relations and armed services committees, and would handle all congressional oversight of intelligence matters.[3]

The Taylor Report, October 1975

As the Murphy Report was reaching the desks of policymakers, a team of six CIA officers, quietly commissioned by DCI William Colby and led by CIA Deputy Comptroller James Taylor,

---

[1] The commission's members were Robert D. Murphy, chairman; David M. Abshire; Anne Armstrong; Rep. William S. Broomfield; William J. Casey; Mrs. Charles E. Engelhard, Jr.; Rep. Peter Frelinghuysen; Arend D. Lubbers; Rep. William S. Mailliard; Sen. Mike Mansfield; Frank C.P. McGlinn; Sen. James B. Pearson; Vice President Nelson Rockefeller; Stanley P. Wagner; and Rep. Clement J. Zablocki.

[2] Commission on the Organization of the Government for the Conduct of Foreign Policy, June 1975, [Final Report] (Washington, DC: Government Printing Office, 1975), 91–92.

[3] Ibid., 99, 100–102 and 208.

submitted its own appraisal of the Intelligence Community in September 1975. Colby passed the Taylor Report along to the President and the NSC without explicitly endorsing its recommendations. Its authors, senior Agency experts and managers, were relatively obscure compared with the congressmen and public figures who served on the Murphy Commission. Since they spoke with considerable candor, DCI Colby nevertheless believed their report worth forwarding despite what he acknowledged was its "CIA perspective."[4]

The Taylor Report urged changes to ease the imbalance between the DCI's mission and authority.

Taylor's CIA study group noted the dilemma that had confounded observers for years—that when the National Security Act had made the DCI responsible in some way for all intelligence, it had not anticipated the technological marvels and accompanying budgetary imperatives that had made the Defense Department the owner of most of America's intelligence collection systems.[5] Writing as the House and Senate investigations of intelligence progressed on Capitol Hill, the authors believed that "political developments" would soon lead Congress to rewrite the National Security Act of 1947. Agreeing that the Act needed revision, they urged their superiors to use this unique opportunity to propose changes that would ease the inefficiency and friction that the imbalance between the DCI's mission and authority inflicted upon the community.[6]

In considering reforms, Taylor and his colleagues assumed that the government needed someone to be "the nation's principal intelligence officer."[7] Such an officer could exist in one of only three forms: as a super-DCI controlling all significant intelligence activities and funds; as a Defense Department official commanding a transferred CIA and most other intelligence functions; or as a DCI speaking with a stronger voice in resource and personnel matters (while State and the Defense Department retained control over their own intelligence activities).[8] They found only the third option feasible, given the "fundamental political and substantive problems" that would surely block the first two.[9]

The question then became one of how to enhance the DCI's powers. Taylor and his colleagues proposed a new-model DCI (which they called a Director General of Intelligence or DGI), who would relinquish line management of CIA in order to concentrate on community affairs. To increase his stature vis-à-vis the Secretaries of State and Defense, this DGI, they suggested, should be made a statutory member of the NSC. While not proposing that the DGI have operational control over all Intelligence Community programs, the Taylor Report offered a way to greatly increase his authority over them. The report proposed that the bulk of the intelligence budget now appropriated to Defense and CIA should instead be appropriated directly to the DGI, for his allocation to the Intelligence Community's program managers.[10]

The Ogilvie Report, November 1975

The Taylor study had few readers, but it indirectly affected discussions in the White House, thanks to its influence on another survey completed that

---

[4] CIA Study Group, "American Intelligence: A Framework for the Future," 13 October 1975. During 1970–1971, Taylor had worked at OMB and helped prepare the 1971 Schlesinger study [Harold P. Ford, *William Colby as Director of Central Intelligence, 1973–1976* (Washington, DC: CIA History Staff, 1993), 19n; the original copy of this study is still classified]. Recollections of those involved identified the authors of the study as Taylor, Richard Lehman, George Carver, William Wells, Gail Donnelly, and Leslie Dirks.
[5] Ibid., 7–8 and 33.
[6] Ibid., 93.
[7] Ibid., 53.
[8] Ibid., iv–v and 60.
[9] Ibid., 50–59.
[10] Ibid., vi–viii, 65–67, and 73.

autumn. In early November 1975 President Gerald Ford chose George H. W. Bush, then chief of the US Liaison Office in Beijing, to succeed William Colby as DCI, and a few days later the President directed his National Security Council to report in a month on the "organization and management of the foreign intelligence community." Ford's motive in commissioning a crash survey at this time is not clear. The Church and Pike Committees' hearings on foreign intelligence begun the previous January were nearing completion, and for several weeks that autumn White House staffers had been drafting a new executive order to govern intelligence activities. A new study would presumably support this effort. The NSC and OMB staffs rapidly organized a team led by Donald G. Ogilvie of OMB and comprising members from across the intelligence and policy community—including James Taylor as its CIA representative.[11]

In keeping with its short deadline, the Ogilvie Report on the Intelligence Community bears marks of haste. National Security Adviser Brent Scowcroft had directed the team to "evaluate the need for changes in the current organization" and to "present options for a possible reorganization."[12] The finished study contended with a minimum of explanation that while the communist target would continue to absorb the bulk of the nation's intelligence resources, in the years to come emerging technologies, international economic troubles, and the proliferation of weapons of mass destruction would complicate the tasks of collection and analysis.[13] Ogilvie and his colleagues noted three areas for improvement:

- Enhancing policy oversight to create proper safeguards against future intelligence abuses;

- Providing better intelligence support to policymakers and military commanders; and

- Ensuring that intelligence activities (from budgeting to covert action) were "well directed."[14]

In their brief treatment the authors made no compelling case for change, but rather listed a wide range of reorganization options and (mutually exclusive) premises about the urgency of intelligence reform.

Having sounded an uncertain trumpet, the Ogilvie team offered no explicit recommendation among the four "major structural options" it described. The options themselves were centralizing in their tendency and ranged from creating a powerful "Director of Intelligence" with line and budget control over all national programs, to a modest modification of the status quo that would enhance the DCI's existing powers.[15] All four options, moreover, assumed that the DCI should relinquish day-to-day management of CIA to head the community with greater or lesser powers in directing its affairs, depending on the option. The report also recommended that the departments should continue to produce intelligence tailored to their own needs.[16]

External events, limitations in the mandates and membership of the Murphy, Taylor, and Ogilvie teams, and their conflicting proposals for change, all served to circumscribe their

The Ogilvie study contended that in the years to come emerging technologies, international economic troubles, and the proliferation of weapons of mass destruction would complicate the tasks of collection and analysis.

---

[11] Draft Report to the President on Organization and Management of the Foreign Intelligence Community, 16 December 1975. The Ogilvie team was called the "Intelligence Organization Group."
[12] Brent Scowcroft, National Security Adviser, to the Secretaries of State, Treasury, and Defense, the Attorney General, the Director, Office of Management and Budget, and the Director of Central Intelligence, "Organization and Management of the Foreign Intelligence Community," 14 November 1975, Community Management Staff Job 79M00476A, box 18, folder 8 (the original of this memo is still classified).
[13] "Organization and Management of the Foreign Intelligence Community," 6–8.
[14] Ibid., 10–21.
[15] Ibid., 2–3.
[16] Ibid., 31.

significance. Moreover, after allegations of serious CIA misconduct had erupted in late 1974, a presidential commission and two congressional investigations of intelligence wrongdoing got under way in January 1975. All this made it hard for the Murphy, Taylor or Ogilvie reports to compete for attention. Still, the three reports contributed both to the Ford administration's response to the congressional investigations and to its decision to follow up on the 1971 Schlesinger Report's recommendation to strengthen the DCI's ability to provide firmer direction for the Intelligence Community. President Ford's Executive Order 11905 of February 1976 moved in this direction by publicly clarifying the DCI's role as community manager and by suggesting that the DCI, "to the extent consistent with his statutory duties, delegate the day-to-day operation of the Central Intelligence Agency" to his DDCI.[17]

---

[17] Gerald R. Ford, Executive Order 11905, United States Intelligence Activities, 18 February 1976, section 3(d)3, reprinted in Michael Warner, ed., *Central Intelligence: Origin and Evolution* (Washington, DC: Central Intelligence Agency, 2001), 93.

The Church and Pike Committee Investigations, 1975–76

The Church Committee, April 1976

The most significant studies of intelligence in the 1970s came from Capitol Hill. In 1975 and 1976, two congressional select committees probed revelations of a host of CIA abuses that first emerged in Seymour Hersh's *New York Times* articles in December 1974. In January 1975 the Senate created a committee to investigate foreign and domestic intelligence activities, including but not limited to allegations of wrongdoing and the adequacy of the laws and oversight mechanisms governing the Intelligence Community. The panel, led by Frank Church (D-ID), interpreted this charter as a mandate to "determine what secret governmental activities are necessary and how they best can be conducted under the rule of law."[1] Church and his colleagues spent 15 months preparing one of the most detailed public appraisals of any nation's intelligence structure.

The Final Report's proposals on the organization and management of the community were articulate and congruent with those of recent executive branch surveys, even down to the idea that the DCI should focus on community affairs and relinquish direct supervision of CIA to a deputy. As a creature of the legislative branch, the committee naturally insisted on greater congressional as well as policymaker oversight of intelligence, and did not hesitate to suggest amendments to the various statutes affecting the field.[2]

The breakthrough for the Church Committee came in its treatment of the operational side of American intelligence. Cost and efficiency, which had preoccupied recent surveys, were not at issue here, but rather the powers and accountability of clandestine activities. The committee suggested that intelligence should be both a collector of data and producer of information, and an instrument for implementing US foreign policy. With its focus on mistakes and misdeeds, the final report concentrated on clandestine activities, but it took a judicious approach that tempered criticisms with a firm conclusion that intelligence had "made important contributions" to national security and become a "permanent and necessary component of our government."[3] This conclusion countered growing public and congressional concern over "the integrity of our nation's intelligence agencies."[4]

The Final Report painted a detailed portrait of clandestine activities, allowing a careful reader to appreciate their several nuances. Espionage, counterintelligence, foreign intelligence liaison, and domestic collection were deemed necessary and valuable, given proper oversight.[5] Even covert action received a grudging endorsement. The committee had considered "proposing a total ban on *all* forms of covert action," but concluded that America should retain a capability to react to extraordinary threats through covert means.[6]

The Pike Committee, early 1976

The Church Committee's success in crafting bipartisan conclusions and winning executive branch assent to issuing a public report stands in contrast to the results of the other congressional study of intelligence conducted at the time. The House Select Committee, chaired by

---

[1] Senate Select Committee to Study Governmental Operations With Respect to Intelligence Activities, "Final Report," Volume 1, "Foreign and Military Intelligence," 94th Congress, Second Session, 1974, 11 and 423. (Cited hereinafter as Church Committee Final Report.)

[2] Ibid., 449. The Final Report shied away from publicly proposing specific changes in the intricate structure of congressional committees to accommodate oversight of intelligence, merely implying that Congress should create one or more "intelligence oversight committee[s]."

[3] Ibid., 1–2 and 424.

[4] Ibid., 423.

[5] Ibid., 437–439 and 459.

[6] Ibid., 159 and 425; emphasis in original.

Otis Pike (D-NY), took an adversarial approach to the Intelligence Community and then complained that the executive branch was stonewalling its inquiry. The full House in early 1976 declined to release the finished report, in effect repudiating the work of its own committee.[7]

Portions of the Pike Committee report nevertheless soon leaked to the press, and the House published its 20-odd recommendations.[8] Many of these recommendations proposed curbs on domestic and foreign operations, including a ban on assassinations and on all covert "paramilitary activities" except in time of war. Its brief proposals on Intelligence Community management included the now-standard suggestion that the DCI be separated from "any of the operating and analytic intelligence agencies" (i.e., from CIA) so he could "be responsible for the supervision and control of all agencies of the United States engaged in foreign intelligence." Just what the DCI's budgetary and administrative powers would be, especially over Defense Department agencies, was not specified. The Pike Committee did offer a detailed proposal for creating a House Permanent Select Committee to oversee domestic and foreign intelligence. The committee also recommended a restraint on the FBI's powers to probe domestic groups suspected of terrorism, and harsh penalties for members of Congress and staffers caught leaking classified information.[9]

Congressional Oversight: Senate and House Intelligence Committees

The practical effects of the two congressional probes took several years to emerge. The most immediate impact was on Congress itself; both chambers soon established permanent select committees to oversee intelligence activities. Although the powers of these committees had distinct limits, thanks in part to their competition with the established authorizing and appropriating committees, they gradually exerted discernible and positive effects on Intelligence Community operations and on its executive branch guidance, tending to make both more disciplined and accountable. Through these committees Congress also began, in the 1980s, to use annual intelligence appropriations to force gradual changes in the Intelligence Community, in essence providing an ongoing reform mechanism that tended for a time to keep a lid on pressures for new surveys. Before the Church and Pike Committee investigations, the Intelligence Community, for practical purposes, was accountable only to the President and the executive branch of government. These investigations, and the formation of the two congressional oversight committees that they inspired, made the Intelligence Community much more accountable to both Congress and the President.

Executive Orders and the Reform Hiatus: 1981–91

In 1978 the Carter administration supplanted President Ford's 1976 Executive Order 11905 with its own Executive Order 12036, which also supported recent recommendations that the DCI take less part in managing the CIA and exert more influence on Intelligence Community affairs.[10] President Carter nevertheless declined to give DCI Stansfield Turner the full scope of authorities he requested to

---

[7] For more on the Pike Committee and its troubles with the White House and the Intelligence Community, see Gerald K. Haines, "The Pike Committee Investigations and the CIA," *Studies in Intelligence* (Winter 1998/99).

[8] New York's *Village Voice* published the leaked portions, which were gathered with commentary and the committee's officially released recommendations as *CIA: The Pike Report* (Nottingham, England: Spokesman Books, 1977). The committee's recommendations are on pages 257–63. The recommendations were also printed in House Select Committee on Intelligence, *Recommendations of the Final Report of the House Select Committee on Intelligence, 94th Congress, 2d Session, 1976.*

[9] *CIA: The Pike Report*, 257–59 and 263.

[10] Jimmy Carter, Executive Order 12036, United States Intelligence Activities, 24 January 1978, reprinted in Warner, *Central Intelligence*, 103ff.

implement this measure. The new Reagan administration sidestepped the issue, and its 1981 Executive Order 12333 generally weakened the DCI's community management powers.[11]

The Reagan and first Bush administrations produced no major surveys of the Intelligence Community. The rapid increase in military and intelligence spending in the Reagan years diminished the earlier interest in cost cutting. Debates over defense reorganization (which culminated in the 1986 Goldwater-Nichols Act), and covert action (which followed the eruption of the Iran-Contra scandal in late 1986), also diverted attention for a time from the task of studying the missions and performance of American intelligence as a whole.

---

[11] Ronald Reagan, Executive Order 12333, United States Intelligence Activities, 4 December 1981, reprinted in Warner, *Central Intelligence*, 127ff.

After the Cold War

The Persian Gulf War and a Revolution in Military Affairs

The 1991 Persian Gulf war demonstrated how developments in weaponry and doctrine were fostering change in warfare and in the warfighters' need for intelligence support. Precision weapons, microprocessing, and real-time, global secure communications were coming together in a military structure now truly capable of joint operations to create what some observers called a "Revolution in Military Affairs."

The Gulf conflict helped to change American intelligence in several ways. First, it exposed weaknesses in the military's and the Intelligence Community's ability to support modern air campaigns. As the Defense Department explained to Congress:

> [The] revolutionary changes in the way American forces conducted combat operations during Operation Desert Storm outstripped the abilities of the [battle damage assessment] system. Analysts were unable to meet the requirements for timely data on a variety of new types of targets or targets struck in new ways.[1]

Secure and computerized communications between operators in Central Command and analysts in the United States partially alleviated this problem; the analysts were able to use national collection resources that had been built for the Cold War to fill some of the tactical intelligence gaps. After the conflict, the White House, Congress, and the Pentagon resolved that battlefield commanders should receive better national and organic intelligence support in future conflicts. Secretary of Defense Richard Cheney took a step toward

this goal in March 1991 when he ordered all of his combatant commanders to create "joint intelligence centers" like that built in Central Command just before the war. Secretary Cheney's decree in effect recognized the military's permanent need for intelligence support at the theater or "operational" level—a requirement that had been overlooked in the separation of "national" from "departmental" intelligence after World War II.[2] The larger problem of how Intelligence Community elements originally formed to assist Washington decisionmakers could also support military operations in the field would prove difficult to resolve, however, and this question would drive many of the debates over intelligence reform in the 1990s and beyond.

The Aspin-Brown Commission, 1995–96

The next full-dress surveys of intelligence did not come until the mid-1990s, some 20 years after the Church and Pike inquiries. By then, the collapse of the Soviet Union and the 1991 war over Kuwait had prompted ongoing debates over national security policy, as well as over reforming (or eliminating) various intelligence functions. Spending cuts in defense and intelligence budgets during the 1990s renewed calls for greater efficiency and provoked arguments over which programs to trim. In the meantime, the continuing evolution of military doctrine after the Gulf war heightened the demand for better battlefield intelligence support. These events, plus the Aldrich Ames spy scandal and a flap over the cost of a new headquarters for the National Reconnaissance Office (NRO), persuaded many members of Congress that the Intelligence Community needed a thorough examination.[3]

---

[1] Office of the Secretary of Defense, *Conduct of the Persian Gulf War* [Pursuant to Title V of the Persian Gulf Supplemental Authorization and Personnel Benefits Act of 1991], (Washington, DC: Department of Defense, 1992), 343.
[2] See Jim Marchio, "The Evolution and Relevance of Joint Intelligence Centers," *Studies in Intelligence* 49, no. 1 (2005): 41–54.
[3] Commission on Roles and Capabilities of the United States Intelligence Community, *Preparing for the 21st Century: An Appraisal of U.S. Intelligence* (Washington, DC: Government Printing Office, 1996), 2. (Hereinafter cited as *Preparing for the 21st Century.)* Loch Johnson has published an account of the work of the commission; see "The Aspin-Brown Intelligence Inquiry: Behind Closed Doors of Blue Ribbon Commission," *Studies in Intelligence* 48, no 3 (2004).

In autumn 1994 Congress authorized a blue-ribbon panel to study the community. The new panel's charter provided for President William J. Clinton to appoint a team of members of Congress and distinguished private citizens (this made the panel's composition similar to the Murphy Commission in the 1970s). With former Defense Secretaries Les Aspin and Harold Brown as its successive chairmen, the "Aspin-Brown Commission" was arguably the highest-ranking group ever to scrutinize the Intelligence Community. This panel and its staff spent 1995 researching and writing a lengthy report, which was publicly released on 1 March 1996.[4]

The Aspin-Brown Commission devoted much of its final report to justifying the continued need for intelligence, even in a post-Cold War world. The report explained that the United States found itself "in a predominant leadership role, whether sought or not." Since the new global order was "likely to be as fraught with peril and uncertainty as the world left behind," American leaders needed the best possible information to maximize the range of choices and the time in which to act.[5] In the commission's view, neither the collection nor the analytical functions of the Intelligence Community were broken, and it thus proposed no radical remedies. Its report nevertheless acknowledged that the community needed help and guidance. While post-Cold War budgets and staffing levels had declined somewhat, personnel costs had climbed to the point where they "crowded out investments in new technologies and limited operational flexibility."[6] What was needed, the report concluded,

was an evolution toward a leaner and more responsive system.

The final report echoed earlier studies in proposing enhanced powers for the Director of Central Intelligence. (These enhanced powers, however, were not to separate him formally from CIA or "to alter the fundamental relationship between the DCI and the Secretary of Defense").[7] As several earlier surveys had proposed, the DCI was to have two deputies: one for the Intelligence Community and one for the "day-to-day" management of CIA. Finally, the DCI should have a larger role in selecting and evaluating the heads of the large Defense Department intelligence agencies and new authority over intelligence personnel systems, as well as improved community budget data and a larger staff to evaluate them.[8]

The Aspin-Brown Commission intimated that important trends were changing the business of intelligence. It even did something that no intelligence survey since the 1948 Eberstadt study had done when it devoted a chapter to the connections between intelligence and law enforcement. The commission found that the two disciplines had different motivations and goals that complicated their dealings. For this reason, National Security Council guidance, as well as improved coordination, were needed to deal with global criminal activity by terrorists, drug traffickers, and others that posed a growing danger to the American public.[9]

The commission's final report also discussed the "radical change in the nature of warfare" wrought by new developments in weaponry and doctrine. The report noted how new weapons

---

[4] Aspin died in May 1995; Brown succeeded him as chairman. Former Senator Warren B. Rudman served as vice chairman and briefly ran the commission in the interregnum before Brown's appointment. The other members of the commission were: Lew Allen, Zoë Baird, Ann Z. Caracristi, Tony Coelho, David H. Dewhurst, Norman D. Dicks, J. James Exon, Wyche Fowler, Jr., Stephan Friedman, Porter J. Goss, Anthony S. Harrington, Robert J. Hermann, Robert E. Pursley, John W. Warner, and Paul D. Wolfowitz. Former Senate Select Committee on Intelligence counsel L. Britt Snider headed the staff.
[5] *Preparing for the 21st Century*, 9–15.
[6] Ibid., 96 and 131.
[7] Ibid., xix and 53–54.
[8] Ibid., 54–57 and 80–81.
[9] Ibid., xviii.

and tactics had increased the Pentagon's demands for intelligence support and wondered whether these demands were really, as President Clinton had recently declared, "the highest priority for US intelligence agencies."[10] The commission nevertheless endorsed the idea of shifting imagery analysis from CIA to a new "National Imagery and Mapping Agency" in the Defense Department to facilitate closer combat support, and it applauded the recent creation of joint intelligence centers at the Unified Commands.[11] The commissioners did not believe, however, that the Defense Department needed "a single authoritative leader for military intelligence." Combining the department's various responsibilities for intelligence "under a single manager would not improve the quality of intelligence support, but would only complicate the performance of the existing roles and responsibilities."[12]

HPSCI's "IC21" Staff Study, 1996

The staff of the House Permanent Select Committee on Intelligence took a novel approach to intelligence reform in that same year. In January 1995 the 104th Congress opened, and the new Republican HPSCI chairman, Larry Combest of Texas, apparently wanted to ensure that the Aspin-Brown Commission—most of whose members President Clinton had appointed—did not have the last word. "A key issue is *opportunity*, not reform," declared the HPSCI staff's April 1996 report (emphasis in original). The HPSCI staff study, "IC21: The Intelligence Community in the 21st Century," thus examined the community with an eye to

explaining where it "needs to be in the next 10-to-15 years." [13]

How the community would get to such a point was problematic, given the problems it currently faced. Indeed, competition among disciplines and agencies had fragmented an intelligence system "that should be highly synergistic."[14] The IC21 Report concentrated on the intelligence collection disciplines, which were not only taking an increasing share of the intelligence budget at the expense of processing and analysis, but also creating an "imbalance in collection management priorities favoring near-term crises at the expense of baseline capabilities and future needs."[15] IC21 argued that the community needed "corporateness" for its agencies and employees "to run, to function and to behave as part of a more closely integrated enterprise."[16] Stronger management, especially in collection, was required to force important cross-program and cross-discipline tradeoffs.[17] Like the Aspin-Brown Report, the IC21 study advocated enhancements in the DCI's powers instead of the creation of a new intelligence coordinator. It wanted to let the existing deputy director of central intelligence run the CIA and to create a second DDCI by statute to handle "community management."

The IC21 study and the Aspin-Brown Report reached opposite conclusions on the issue of appointing a chief for all intelligence in the Defense Department:

> *Enhancing the DCI's authority solves some, but not all, of the problems. It is important that the defense intelligence*

The IC21 study and the Aspin-Brown Report reached opposite conclusions on the issue of appointing a chief for all intelligence in the Defense Department.

---

[10] Ibid., 21–22.
[11] Ibid., 109, 124.
[12] Ibid., 111–112.
[13] House Permanent Select Committee on Intelligence, "IC21: The Intelligence Community in the 21st Century," 104th Congress, Second Session, 1996, 1–2 (hereinafter cited as IC21). HPSCI Staff Director Mark M. Lowenthal led the IC21 effort.
[14] Ibid., 8–9 and 23.
[15] Ibid., 97.
[16] Ibid., 8.
[17] Ibid., 97.

establishment also have a single official who is both responsible for and empowered to address [organizational] issues, or to advise the SECDEF about them.

The study's authors therefore recommended that the director of the Defense Intelligence Agency should be given a new title as "Director of Military Intelligence" and new authority to coordinate Defense Department intelligence budgets, as well as an Assistant Secretary of Defense for Intelligence to advise the secretary on policy, planning, and oversight matters.[18] The study also contained a host of other organizational adjustments, such as its proposal to lift the CIA's Directorate of Operations out of the Agency and subordinate it directly to the DCI, and to merge the NSA, NRO, and various other collection organizations in a "Technical Collection Agency" under the Secretary of Defense and the proposed DDCI for community management.[19]

Congress merged divergent proposals from these two studies in crafting the Intelligence and Defense Authorization Acts for fiscal year 1997, enacting them as amendments to the National Security Act of 1947. The revised Act now gave the DCI a new DDCI for Community Management, along with three "Assistant Directors of Central Intelligence" to coordinate collection, administration, and analysis and production. The community's imagery interpretation offices were merged in a National Imagery and Mapping Agency (NIMA) under the Secretary of Defense. The DCI also received more clout over defense intelligence budgets

A survey of the challenges and opportunities facing intelligence seemed a logical complement to work being done in the Pentagon.

as well as influence in the appointments of directors of the NSA, NRO, and DIA.

The Scowcroft Review of Intelligence, 2001

While the Clinton administration had been content to allow these changes and its own restatement of intelligence priorities (in Presidential Decision Directive 35 of March 1995) to work their effects in its second term, the incoming administration felt a need to take a fresh look at the Intelligence Community. In part this impetus stemmed from Secretary of Defense Donald Rumsfeld's initial efforts to transform the nation's military; a survey of the challenges and opportunities facing intelligence seemed a logical complement to the work being done in the Pentagon. In May 2001 President George W. Bush authorized such a study in National Security Presidential Directive 5, tapping Brent Scowcroft (who had been his father's national security adviser) to lead the blue-ribbon panel.[20]

The attacks of 11 September 2001 soon diverted the policymaker and community attention that the Scowcroft panel required to complete its work. The study that the panel drafted and signed has not been publicly released or circulated even within the Intelligence Community. Press accounts suggest that its final version called for creation of a collection management agency like that proposed in IC21, but placed under the DCI. Such a step, which would amount to the largest single enlargement of DCI authority since President Truman created the position in 1946, was reportedly strongly opposed by Secretary of

---

[18] Ibid., 16, 62–63.

[19] Ibid., 20 and 23–24.

[20] George W. Bush, National Security Presidential Directive (NSPD) 5, "Intelligence," 9 May 2001. The other members of the panel were cochairman Adm. David Jeremiah, USN (Ret.), John S. Foster, Jamie Gorelick, Richard J. Kerr, Jeong Kim, Amb. J. Stapleton Roy, and William Schneider Jr. NSPD-5 also directed the DCI to appoint another panel of "members of the Intelligence Community and other senior United States Government officials" to conduct an "independent, but parallel" study. That panel, which suspended its work after 11 September, was headed by Deputy Director of Central Intelligence for Community Management Joan Dempsey and comprised the deputy directors of the major intelligence agencies. A single staff, headed by Kevin Scheid and Howard Schue, served both panels. One of the coauthors of this present monograph served on that staff.

Defense Donald Rumsfeld.[21] The Scowcroft review may have had at least one indirect effect. In April 2003, Secretary Rumsfeld took a step to strengthen and consolidate the administration of the Defense Department's intelligence capabilities, creating the statutory post of Under Secretary of Defense (Intelligence) to replace the Assistant Secretary of Defense for Command, Control, Communications and Intelligence (C³I) as the secretary's principal adviser on intelligence matters. The new USD(I) resembled the overall defense intelligence secretaries proposed by IC21 and earlier by the 1971 Schlesinger Report.

The 9/11 Commission Report, 2004

The events on 11 September also prompted calls for high-level investigations of what had happened to make such a catastrophe possible. Two such inquiries offered comprehensive reviews of the Intelligence Community's performance and received widespread attention. By far the most important of these was the independent National Commission on Terrorist Attacks Upon the United States (better known as the 9/11 Commission), established by an act of Congress in late 2002.[22] Indeed, in absolute terms the 9/11 Commission may have devoted more attention and resources to studying the community than had some of the blue-ribbon panels discussed earlier. In any event, its findings and proposals have proven more influential than any of them.

The 9/11 commissioners and staff built upon the findings of an earlier investigation, Congress' "Joint Inquiry" into the Intelligence Community's activities with regard to the 9/11 attacks. That inquiry had presented a host of findings and recommendations in December 2002, one of which was for the appointment of a Director of National Intelligence separated from the day-to-day management of the CIA, who would hold expanded budgetary and administrative authorities to run the Intelligence Community.[23] While the 9/11 Commission conducted its work over the next 18 months, several congressmen introduced bills to implement proposals similar to those drafted by the joint inquiry.[24]

From its inception, the 9/11 Commission worked in a glare of publicity that actually helped it gain access to senior officials and sensitive documentation. The commissioners took public testimony (some of it under oath) and heard briefings on a wide range of intelligence topics. Its well-written report, released on 22 July 2004, almost instantly became a bestseller, and thus its findings and recommendations on intelligence (themselves only a portion of the larger work) received a wide audience. The timing of the report's release—in the midst of a presidential election season—only heightened the attention paid to the commission's proposals, and gave both Congress and the White House further incentives to support some form of intelligence reform.

The timing of the 9/11 Report's release—in the midst of a presidential election season—heightened the attention paid to its proposals, and gave Congress and the White House further incentives to support some form of intelligence reform.

---

[21] Walter Pincus, "Intelligence Shakeup Would Boost CIA," *Washington Post*, 8 November 2001; Walter Pincus, "Rumsfeld Casts Doubt on Intelligence Reform," *Washington Post*, 9 April 2002.

[22] The commission was established as an entity of the legislative branch by the Intelligence Authorization Act for Fiscal Year 2003 (PL 107–306), which passed on 27 November 2002. It was chaired by former New Jersey Governor Thomas H. Kean, and its vice chairman was retired Congressman Lee H. Hamilton. Its members were Richard Ben-Veniste, Fred F. Fielding, Jamie S. Gorelick, Slade Gorton, Bob Kerrey, John F. Lehman, Timothy J. Roemer, and James R. Thompson. The staff director was Philip Zelikow. See *The 9/11 Commission Report*, (Washington, DC: Government Printing Office, 2004). There was some overlap between the personnel of the 9/11 Commission and the earlier Scowcroft Commission; Jamie Gorelick, for instance, served on both panels, as did several members of the staff (most notably Kevin Scheid).

[23] Senate Select Committee on Intelligence and House Permanent Select Committee on Intelligence, "Joint Inquiry Into Intelligence Community Activities Before and After the Terrorist Attacks of September 11, 2001," 107th Congress, 2nd Session, December 2002; see Recommendation 1.

[24] A good example of these was HR 4104, the "Intelligence Transformation Act of 2004," offered by the minority members of the House Permanent Select Committee on Intelligence on 1 April 2004.

The 9/11 Commission's Report proposed sweeping change in the Intelligence Community. Some of its suggestions echoed those of earlier surveys. The DCI's duties, for instance, should be split between a chief of the Intelligence Community (the National Intelligence Director, or NID) and a director of the CIA. Under the commission's proposals, the new NID would wield full authority over the National Foreign Intelligence Program budget, which would come to him or her in a separate appropriation. Other recommendations were more novel. For instance, the NID would supervise three deputy NIDs for homeland security, defense intelligence, and foreign intelligence, each of whom would also hold joint appointments as senior deputies in the FBI, the Defense Department, and the CIA, respectively. Perhaps the commission's most original proposal was for domestic and foreign terrorism analysis and "strategic planning" to be done by a National Counterterrorism Center (NCTC), under the NID's authority. The NCTC would be a hybrid organization to bridge—at least with regard to terrorism—the divides between foreign and domestic intelligence, and between intelligence and law enforcement, that had been decreed by the National Security Act in 1947.[25]

President Bush adopted several of the 9/11 Commission Report's proposals a month later, signing four Executive Orders on intelligence and related issues.[26] Executive Order 13355, "Strengthened Management of the Intelligence Community," gave the DCI marginally more authority than he had ever held. It did so by updating Executive Order 12333 (December 1981) to reflect subsequent changes to the National Security Act and by emphasizing the DCI's responsibility to exercise his powers to the maximum extent of the law. Executive Order 13355 emphasized the director's duty to provide intelligence against all threats to the United States (whether that intelligence originated from sources at home or abroad), to ensure the integration of Intelligence Community activities, and to create "national centers" to work on high-priority intelligence topics. The DCI received new authority to monitor the Defense Department's spending on tactical intelligence and to concur in the appointments and tenure of the heads of other intelligence organizations. Executive Order 13355, mild as it was, represented perhaps the most that any White House could unilaterally do toward empowering the DCI to manage the Intelligence Community. Indeed, the White House portrayed it as an interim step toward a true chief of national intelligence while Congress was considering legislation to amend the National Security Act.[27]

By early October 2004, the House and Senate had separately passed wholesale amendments to the National Security Act. Both of these lengthy bills included somewhat disparate elements for the purpose of garnering broad support in their respective chambers. The Senate's bill hewed fairly closely to the 9/11 Commission's recommendations, especially in separating the new head of the community from day-to-day supervision of the CIA, but it created a more streamlined administrative apparatus for the new director than the commission had proposed, rejecting the idea of jointly appointed deputies and the commission's suggestion that the director be part of the Executive Office of the President.[28] The

[25] *The 9/11 Commission Report*, 403–406, 411–14.
[26] The Executive Orders were "Establishing the President's Board on Safeguarding Americans' Civil Liberties" (EO 13353); "National Counterterrorism Center" (EO 13354); "Strengthened Management of the Intelligence Community" (EO 13355); and "Strengthening the Sharing of Terrorism Information to Protect Americans" (EO 13356). All were signed on 27 August 2004.
[27] A "senior administration official" on 27 August told reporters that the four Executive Orders made up a sort of "down payment on the President's enduring commitment to work with Congress to establish the National Intelligence Director, which must be done by statute." See the full text of the press conference at "White House Conference Call Background Briefing [on] President's Executive Orders," Federal News Service, 27 August 2004.
[28] The Senate's bill, S. 2845, was titled the "National Intelligence Reform Act of 2004." The House's HR 10 was known as the "9/11 Recommendations Implementation Act."

House's version also created a Director of National Intelligence, but reserved more powers for the Secretary of Defense and included a range of antiterror provisions not strictly related to intelligence reform.

Once both bills had received affirmative votes, the House and Senate appointed conferees to reconcile the many differences between them in a single text for final passage. Negotiations were intense, and in some respects echoed the debates over the original National Security Act in 1947.[29] They essentially pitted concerns over civil liberties and support to military operations against a broad desire to ensure that the overall coordinator of US intelligence—now called the Director of National Intelligence—could prosecute the War on Terror and make the 15 intelligence agencies work as a team. A final text did not emerge until after President Bush won reelection in early November. The House and Senate worked into the final hours of the 108th Congress before passing the "Intelligence Reform and Terrorism Prevention Act of 2004" on 8 December. President Bush signed it into law nine days later.

The new act marked the end of the road for the position of Director of Central Intelligence and a quiet revision of one of the fundamental compromises struck by the drafters of the original National Security Act. While reporters narrated the arguments between House and Senate over the precise budgetary and tasking authorities to give the Director of National Intelli-

gence, other important issues were being settled with little fanfare.

The Intelligence Reform and Terrorism Prevention Act incorporated the 9/11 Commission's notion that American intelligence needed a new sort of coordinator: one who would manage the community across the full range of intelligence, foreign and domestic. One key to this development was the act's redefinition of "national" intelligence as "all intelligence, regardless of the source from which derived and including information gathered within and outside the United States."[30] The Truman administration and the 80th Congress in 1947 had made domestic and foreign intelligence into separate realms, but now the new DNI would bridge them. He or she would have better tools to use in building such a bridge, from new authority to establish common technology and security standards for community information systems to a National Counterterrorism Center—an idea initially lifted from the 9/11 Commission's Report. The NCTC would work for the DNI to serve as the nation's primary organization for analysis of foreign-sponsored terrorism and to plan and assign counterterrorism roles and responsibilities to the departments and agencies to perform under their own unique authorities.[31]

This shift in emphasis for the overall coordinator of intelligence appealed to lawmakers in part because it removed the DNI from day-to-day management of CIA and precluded any

Key to the new DNI's power was the Intelligence Reform and Terrorism Prevention Act's redefinition of national intelligence.

---

[29] Perhaps the clearest echo was the concern among military officials and congressional allies that commanders would not be able to rely on a civilian intelligence agency or director for crucial battlefield support. A good summary of the background and course of the congressional debates over intelligence reform is contained in Richard A. Best, Jr., "Intelligence Community Reorganization: Potential Effects on DOD Intelligence Agencies," Library of Congress, Congressional Research Service, 6 December 2004, 14–17.

[30] See Section 1012 of the Act. This language replaced the definition in Section 3(5) of the National Security Act (as amended), which had said that "national intelligence" by and large did "not refer to counterintelligence or law enforcement activities" conducted by the FBI.

[31] See Section 102A(g) of the National Security Act of 1947 as amended by Section 1011 of the Intelligence Reform and Terrorism Prevention Act of 2004, along with Section 1021 of that Act. Section 1011 was a large portion of the 2004 Act devoted to the DNI and his span of control over the Intelligence Community.

clandestine operating role for the DNI's organization. Not a few members of Congress over the course of 2004 insisted that such a separation was a sine qua non of intelligence reform.[32] The act split the DNI from CIA, which would ultimately be responsible to him but would keep its foreign intelligence collection and covert action duties.[33] The DNI would have no unvouchered funds, however, and thus could not run clandestine operations of his own (or at least could not run them effectively).[34] The DNI's operational role would thus be in supervising the planning, policy, and budgets of the Intelligence Community.

In the new intelligence structure, the President and Congress replaced the DCI with a DNI. Since 1947 the DCI had sought to provide strategic warning and to serve as a clearinghouse for overseas operations, while also overseeing the community. The DNI will now oversee the community and provide strategic warning, while delegating the conduct of operations to the executing agencies. The new law thus bridges the foreign-domestic divide from the 1947 National Security Act. The divide, nevertheless, is likely to endure unless the nation's strategic or political circumstances change dramatically.

---

[32] For example, Sen. Dianne Feinstein (D-CA) complained in a July 2004 hearing that the CIA had "abused its unique position in the intelligence community" (during analytical debates over Iraq) and that the "two very different" jobs of director of the CIA and director of the Intelligence Community were too much for any single official and therefore must be split into two positions. "Even if one extraordinary person could manage the workload of both jobs," she argued, "they are inherently incompatible." See Federal News Service, "Hearing of the Senate Select Committee on Intelligence," 20 July 2004, 7.

[33] For the issue of the DNI's oversight of CIA, see, for instance, Sec. 102A(f)4; Sec. 102A(k); Sec. 102A(r); Sec. 104A(b), and Sec. 104A(d)4 of the National Security Act of 1947 as amended by Section 1011 of the Intelligence Reform and Terrorism Prevention Act of 2004.

[34] See Sec. 102A(n) of the National Security Act of 1947 as amended by Section 1011 of the Intelligence Reform and Terrorism Prevention Act of 2004.

Conclusions

Our survey of intelligence reform studies is neither a comprehensive summary of reorganization proposals nor a chronology of the Intelligence Community's evolution since World War II. It rather examines some of the best-informed and insightful thinking over almost 60 years about how the community works as a system, and how it might be improved. It thus provides an opportunity to review the judgments of senior officials and experts who enjoyed broad access to sensitive information and files and searched diligently for ways to bolster America's security. The sense of déjà vu that the knowledgeable reader may feel in reading this account is a hint of the importance of studying the reports of the reform commissions; by wrestling with the "eternal questions," these surveys leave us better prepared to ponder similar questions today.

When we examine why some intelligence surveys produced change while others did not, we have to conclude that it is by no means entirely a matter of their merit, whether judged at the time or in retrospect. Change can be deliberately planned or basically reactive. It is usually a little of both, since the best thought-out proposal for reform can be affected by such factors as personalities, timing, political influence, and events in the world at large. Indeed, change in the Intelligence Community emerges in many ways. Some changes come about by presidential order, congressional action, or interagency agreement, while others result from the demands of new technology or the need to accommodate allies.

While a good deal of change in the Intelligence Community has been more random and ad hoc than systematically planned, the bureaucratic impetus to commission a thorough study when contemplating change is almost inexorable. To bring significant change to the Intelligence Community, a study commission has had to get two things right: process and substance.

Process

The studies that changed the community have usually shared some or all of the following characteristics:

- **Sponsorship by the White House or Congress.** Two studies that had large and comparatively rapid effects—the 1949 Dulles Report and the 1971 Schlesinger Report—were both commissioned by the National Security Council at a time when it was dissatisfied with its intelligence support. Two surveys commissioned by Congress had major impacts: the reports of the Church Committee and the 9/11 Commission. Sponsorship by elected officials, of course, does not guarantee a high degree of influence: the Pike Committee worked at the same time as Senator Church's panel but achieved little or nothing, and the NSC's Scowcroft Commission saw its work eclipsed by the events of 11 September 2001. Reports and studies generated within the Intelligence Community itself, however, have uniformly had little effect.

- **Undertaken in conjunction with a war.** Studies whose findings emerge while American troops are in combat, or just after, are more likely to result in change. Indeed, a war usually broadens the range of possible intelligence reforms. The drafters of the National Security Act in 1947 drew lessons from the greatest war in history to construct a new postwar security system. The outbreak of the Korean War in 1950 brought about the intelligence reforms proposed by the Dulles Report and tentatively approved by the NSC over a year earlier. The 1971 Schlesinger Report responded to the need to cut spending as President Nixon extracted the United States from the long and costly Vietnam War. The 9/11 Commission Report, of course, was prompted by the costliest attacks on American soil in living memory and written as the War on Terror and operations in Iraq ground on.

Studies whose recommendations would cause power in the Intelligence Community to gravitate either towards the DCI or the Secretary of Defense—or both—have generally had the most influence and are the most likely to be implemented.

- **Prepared concurrently with other studies.** Surveys conducted nearly simultaneously often amplify each other's influence. There have been several such conjunctions: the Eberstadt Report arrived within weeks of the influential Dulles Report in early 1949. In 1975, the Murphy Commission study and the Taylor and Ogilvie Reports affected President Ford's response (especially in drafting Executive Order 11905) to the Church and Pike probes in Congress, which together prompted Congress to establish permanent intelligence oversight committees. The 9/11 Commission's Report drew from the work of the recent Scowcroft Commission and Congressional probes into 9/11 and Iraq.

- **Well-informed, well-argued, and well-written.** Reports prepared by knowledgeable parties with good access to data, a sound analytical framework, and clear prose have been more likely to find a favorable reception. James Schlesinger's 1971 report to the NSC, for example, revealed formidable analytic power and a keen rhetorical edge; both undoubtedly enhanced its influence. The 9/11 Commission's compelling report was a national bestseller. On the other hand, the HPSCI staff's long and rambling 1996 IC21 study, while well-informed, would have profited from more rigorous editorial discipline. Of all the studies examined, the 1955 Clark Task Force Report displays, in its leaden prose, the least insight into the Intelligence Community. (It is worth noting that studies prepared for short deadlines, such as the 1975 Ogilvie Report, suffer from their haste; the better studies usually take at least a year to generate.)

- **Led by future DCIs.** The report of a study commission whose chairman later becomes DCI, as in the case of Allen Dulles and James Schlesinger (who was also later Secretary of Defense), is likely to have a lasting impact. The new DCI is likely to use his experience on the commission as a touchstone in evaluating community affairs, and as a template for making changes.

Substance

In the substance of these reports, one large trend is evident over the years. Studies such as the Dulles and Schlesinger Reports, whose recommendations would cause power in the Intelligence Community to gravitate either towards the Director of Central Intelligence or the Office of the Secretary of Defense—or both—have generally had the most influence and are the most likely to be implemented. Studies tended to make a difference if they reinforced this long-term trend to increase the concentration of power over intelligence in the hands of both the DCI and—later and more slowly—the Secretary of Defense. This pattern endured from the late 1940s into 2004, regardless of whether Democrats or Republicans controlled the White House or Congress. The losers in this trend were the Department of State, the armed services, and, to a lesser extent, the Joint Chiefs of Staff. Until early in the Cold War, these institutions had dominated American intelligence; they soon did so no longer.

The 9/11 Commission Report and the legislation that it midwifed broke this pattern and established a new one that is likely to prove enduring. The double shock of 11 September 2001 and the community's misestimate of Iraqi weapons programs had convinced Congress, the president, and the public that American intelligence had to be made both better integrated and more accountable. The answer to both requirements, it seemed, was to appoint one official—a Director of National Intelligence—to ensure that all three of the responsibilities that had accrued to the Director of Central Intelligence (i.e., providing strategic warning, coordinating clandestine activities, and managing the performance of the Intelligence Community) were performed effectively across both the foreign and domestic intelligence realms. The DNI, it was hoped, would have full authority to oversee all intelligence regarding the safety of the United States. The emphasis on integrating foreign and domestic intelligence work was the key to the change; it has set the DNI in a position metaphorically equidistant between the defense establishment and the less-defined federal capability to defend the American homeland. Where there were two main focuses of power in the Intelligence Community before 2004—the DCI and the Secretary of Defense—there are now three, including the homeland security mission.

Reform and the Constitution

What do these studies tell us about the larger course of intelligence transformation? Sweeping intelligence reform is rare because it is so difficult. To make more than incremental change, the US Constitution requires broad cooperation by two entire branches of government—Congress, which diffuses its two houses' authority among their committees, and the Executive Branch, whose departments each respond to different political and institutional pressures. Within the Executive Branch, the Intelligence Community itself is a confederation of disparate agencies. The studies we have examined nonetheless reveal that, despite these systemic difficulties, reform is possible when most of the key political and bureaucratic actors agree that something must change—even if they do not all agree on exactly what that change should be. Studies of the Intelligence Community can help create agreement on the need for change if they are seen as both timely and authoritative—i.e., representative, logical and judicious. Even a study that offers little new information can bolster intelligence reform if it shows policymakers a responsible alternative to what already exists.

Intelligence reform efforts and blue-ribbon studies of the Intelligence Community will resume, of course, perhaps soon after the President and Congress have implemented the Intelligence Reform and Terrorism Prevention Act of 2004. Intelligence is too large, too complicated, and too important either to fix at a stroke or to leave alone. What is new, however, is the changed institutional dynamic that has emerged since the 11 September 2001 attacks and the passage of the act. It remains to be seen which department or agency will take the lead in providing intelligence support for the homeland security mission, and how effective the new DNI will be in working with it. In the search for new solutions, perhaps some advanced by earlier intelligence reform studies will find new validity. While the shape of the 2004 act's new settlement remains uncertain, the DNI clearly will need a host of imaginative solutions to cope with old problems and new tensions as he balances traditional intelligence needs against the unprecedented and competing requirements of homeland security.

Intelligence is too large, too complicated, and too important either to fix at a stroke or to leave alone.